45¢

I BELONG TO

PACK 48

DEN 1

MY NAME IS ________

I PLAN TO JOIN

TROOP ________

LION WEBELOS

CUB SCOUT BOOK

PRINTED IN U.S.A. 200M257
NO. 3232 — 45 CENTS

B O Y   S C O U T S   O F   A M E R I C A

NEW BRUNSWICK NEW JERSEY

C O N T

THE BIGGEST YEAR OF ALL 4

HOW TO JOIN 4

CUB SCOUT PROMISE 6

LAW OF THE PACK 7

YOUR DEN 11

YOUR PACK 12

A C H I E V E M E N T S

1. Muscle Builders 13
2. Flag Ceremonies 16
3. Keeping Strong 20
4. Religious Service 22
5. Tools 24
6. Using Your Collection 28
7. Log Book 30
8. Using Rope 32
9. Outdoor Safety 34
10. Family Fun 36
11. Travel From Home 38
12. Storytelling 40

E N T S

ELECTIVES

1. Signals 46
2. Puppets and Things 50
3. Craftsman 54
4. Radio 58
5. Electrician 60
6. Boat Builder 63
7. Sky Observer 68
8. Things That Go 72
9. Mechanic 74
10. Party Giver 78
11. Indian Dancer 82
12. Musician 90
13. Masks 92
14. Photos 95
15. Nature 97
16. Dogs 101
17. Landscaper 104
18. Soil and Water Conservation 106
19. Outdoor Chef 109
20. Shelters 112
21. Swimming 114
22. Safety Service 118
23. Sports 120

BOOKS FOR CUB SCOUTS 126

MORE THINGS TO DO 128

W E B E L O S

You and Boy Scouting 134

Your New Uniform 138

Your Scoutmaster 140

Your Patrol 140

Your Troop 142

A New Ladder to Climb 144

Webelos Requirements 146

Webelos Activities or Preparation for Scouting 158

A WORD TO PARENTS

You have probably noticed your son's need for strenuous physical activity as you have watched him grow up—as he rushed breathlessly from place to place he never walked when he could run, he never ran when he could jump, nor jumped when he could do something more strenuous. The peak of variety in individual play activities will be reached this year.

He will take more interest in organized games, develop a sense of teamwork and be more loyal to his teams.

Your son's imagination and his desire for facts will find an outlet in books of travel, stories of other lands, mechanics and biography, and adventure. Science and nature stories, too, will become increasingly popular.

Most 10-year-old boys still like to collect things and you can help your son by suggesting better ways of using his collection.

A boy of this age gains more and more satisfaction from his ability to achieve.

Give him an opportunity to participate in family decisions, encourage him to complete the Lion requirements and to work on his electives before he becomes 10½, so that he can start right in on his Webelos when he becomes old enough.

the BIGGEST year of all

You are starting the last grand year of Cub Scouting. You'll find it the best year of all, because you will be doing bigger things and be getting ready to become a Boy Scout.

Go right after your Lion achievements so you can get your Lion badge quickly. Then you will still have time for some Arrow Point fun.

When you are 10½ you will want to be ready to earn your Webelos badge. It is the highest rank in Cub Scouting, and it is all about getting ready to be a Boy Scout.

HOW TO JOIN

If you are ten years old and just starting Cub Scouting, the first thing you do is to earn the Bobcat badge. Here are the five things you do to earn it:

1. Learn and give the Cub Scout Promise.
2. Say the Law of the Pack. Tell what it means.
3. Tell what Webelos means.
4. Show the Cub Scout sign and handshake. Tell what they mean.
5. Give the Cub Scout Motto and salute. Tell what they mean.

These five things are explained on the following pages. Ask your mother or dad to read them, too.

NOW—you're on your way!

BOBCAT REQUIREMENTS

When you complete your Bobcat tests, you may do either of two things:

1. You may start with your Wolf and Bear achievements and earn your Wolf and Bear badges, *then* begin your Lion achievements.

OR

2. You may start right out on your Lion achievements and earn your Lion badge. If you do this you will not receive your Wolf or Bear badge, but you will get a quicker start toward becoming a Boy Scout.

When you have become a Bobcat you will be given your Bobcat pin. Wear it only on your everyday clothes, not on your Cub Scout uniform. This pin shows that you are a new Cub Scout.

CUB SCOUT SIGN

The sign is made with your right hand held high and straight up above your shoulder. This is the sign of the Cub Scout all over the world. The two extended fingers stand for the two parts of the Promise.

THE CUB SCOUT PROMISE

I . . . . promise
to DO MY BEST

to do my DUTY
to GOD
and my COUNTRY

to be SQUARE

and to OBEY the
Law of the Pack

 E  E  O 

THE LAW OF THE PACK

The Cub Scout
FOLLOWS Akela

The Cub Scout
HELPS the Pack go

The Pack HELPS
the Cub Scout grow

The Cub Scout
GIVES good will

 E  E  O 

CUB SCOUT PROMISE

I, (say your name), promise
To DO MY BEST
To do my DUTY to GOD
And my COUNTRY
To BE SQUARE, and
To OBEY the Law of the Pack.

When you promise to do something, you mean you will do it. Even if it is hard, a Cub Scout keeps his promise. He wants people to believe him.

When you say, "I will DO MY BEST," you mean, "I will try as hard as I can." One boy's best can be better than another boy's best. Cub Scout leaders do not expect you to be perfect, but they want you to do your best.

When you do your DUTY, you do your share. You do what you ought to do.

Your duty to GOD is done with God's help. It means you practice your religion at home, in the church or synagogue, in everything you do.

Your duty to your COUNTRY means being a good American. Our country's laws take care of the rights that God gives to everybody in the world.

Be SQUARE means being fair to everybody. Sometimes this is not easy. But a Cub Scout will try to be square. He wants everybody to be fair to him, so he is fair to everybody.

The Law of the Pack has four ideas for a Cub Scout to use every day. When you use these ideas, you OBEY the Law of the Pack. Read the explanation of the Law on the next page.

Talk with your parents about the Cub Scout Promise and Law of the Pack. Ask your Den Mother to talk with your Den about the Promise and Law.

LAW OF THE PACK

"The Cub Scout Follows Akela"

Who is Akela?

Akela is the Cub Scout name for a *good leader*. A leader is someone you follow. Some of the people you may call Akela are your father or mother, your teacher, your Den Chief, your Den Mother, your Cubmaster, or anybody who is a good leader.

Most good leaders first learned to follow. That's why the first part of the Law of the Pack asks you to learn to follow. Follow good leaders. Follow Akela.

"The Cub Scout Helps the Pack Go"

When you become a Cub Scout, you are no longer just a boy. Now you are a member of a Den and a Pack. You can't think only of yourself, but you must think of your fellow Cub Scouts.

Help the Pack GO by coming to all meetings, by following the leaders, and by making your Pack better in every way because you are in it.

"The Pack Helps the Cub Scout Grow"

You will have a lot of fun when you join the Pack. You will learn things from other people, and you will learn to do things with them—that's real fun. You help the Pack GO, and the Pack helps you GROW.

"The Cub Scout Gives Good Will"

You will find that if you smile at your friends, they will smile back at you. If you are friendly to them, they will be friendly to you.

Look for things to do for other people. They need not be big jobs but just little things that help.

Smile and *help* — these are two fine Cub Scouting words.

THE HANDSHAKE

When you shake hands with another Cub Scout, hold out your right hand just as you usually would to shake hands, but put your first two fingers along the inside of the other fellow's wrist. This means that he, too, is square and obeys the Law of the Pack.

THE MOTTO

DO YOUR BEST

"DO YOUR BEST." That's the Cub Scout Motto. Another boy may do something better than you do it, but if you do your best you need not be ashamed.

THE SALUTE

Hold your fingers as you do for the sign, except that your first two fingers are closed together. Salute your leaders and other Cub Scouts to show them good will and courtesy.

CUB SCOUT CODE

BUC TUOCS EDOC

If you are a Cub Scout, you can write a letter to another Cub Scout that only you and he can read. Here is the Cub Scout Code:

GNITIRWSDRAWKCAB

That's right — you guessed it! It's writing backwards.

THE LIVING CIRCLE

You usually do the living circle with the other fellows of your Den. Hold out your left hand with your thumb extended and grasp the thumb of the boy on your left. Hold your right hand up in the Cub Scout sign.

The living circle means that all Cub Scouts are friends.

YOUR DEN

YOUR DEN

Is a group of boys in your neighborhood with whom you play. You will meet with them one afternoon a week and have a lot of fun.

YOUR DEN CHIEF

Is a Boy Scout who will help you in your Den.

YOUR DENNER

Is one of the Cub Scouts elected to help the Den Chief.

YOUR DEN MOTHER

Is a Cub Scout's mother who helps plan Den fun.

YOUR DEN DAD

Helps your Den Mother and Cubmaster in many ways, such as planning dad and son outings.

YOUR PACK

WHAT IS A PACK?

A Pack is a group of Dens. Your Pack will meet one evening each month. It is for you and your parents.

YOUR CUBMASTER

Your Cubmaster is a man who spends a lot of time planning and leading your Pack meeting. He meets with your Den Chiefs and Den Mothers and helps them plan your Den meetings.

YOUR PACK COMMITTEE

Is a group of men who help the Cubmaster. They have regular meetings and plan special Pack fun. Your Den Dad is a member of this Committee.

YOUR PACK MEETING

You will have fun during the month getting ready to help put on a show at the Pack meeting. Get to the meeting early to help set up your Den exhibits. These exhibits show everybody what you have done during the month. While the Cubmaster is meeting with your mothers and dads, you will get ready to put on your Den stunt.

AKELA'S COUNCIL

At each Pack meeting the Cub Scouts who have earned badges during the month will receive them in a special ceremony. Your mother and dad will be in this ceremony with you and give your badge to you.

MUSCLE BUILDERS

ACHIEVEMENT 1

Complete any three of the following:

1. Lie on your back, hold your feet down (or hook them under something like a bureau, or fence), then do 20 "sit up" exercises.
2. Play a game of "hangtag" with members of your Den.
3. Do two pull-ups on a bar or six push-ups from the ground or floor.
4. Do a running broad jump of at least seven feet, or 1½ times your height.
5. Jump into water over your head, level off and swim 45 feet, turn over on your back and rest in floating position for 15 seconds, then swim back to starting point. Do this with a grown-up who swims well.

W.E.C. – 11-9-57

MOTHER OR DAD SIGN HERE

The first Lion stunt is a real muscle builder. Start early. When you get tired, it's time to stop. Add a few more times to your record every day. Try the bar pull-ups or the push-ups or the swimming achievement to develop your body. You'll want to be alert, quick, and ready when your team needs you.

SIT UPS
Lie flat. Raise your body slowly. Try to touch toes, keeping legs straight. Work up to 20 gradually.
PUSH UPS
Hold body and arms stiff, hands flat on floor. Lower yourself toward floor, touching with chest. Now up again.
CHINNING BAR
Grasp bar firmly, knuckles away from you. Pull yourself up until your chin is just above bar.

HANG TAG

"It" tries to tag any other fellow who is not quick enough to find something to hang onto.

NOTE TO PARENTS:

Where a licensed physician certifies that Cub Scout's physical condition for an indeterminable time doesn't permit him to do three of the requirements in this achievement, the Cubmaster and the Pack Committee may authorize substitutions of any three of the Arrow Point electives.

FLAG CEREMONIES

ACHIEVEMENT 2

1. Show how to fold the Flag.
2. Draw flags of five nations you are interested in. Hang these drawings with an American Flag in your room or put them in your scrapbook.
3. Help lead a Pack flag ceremony.

VRC - 12-12 - 57

MOTHER OR DAD SIGN HERE

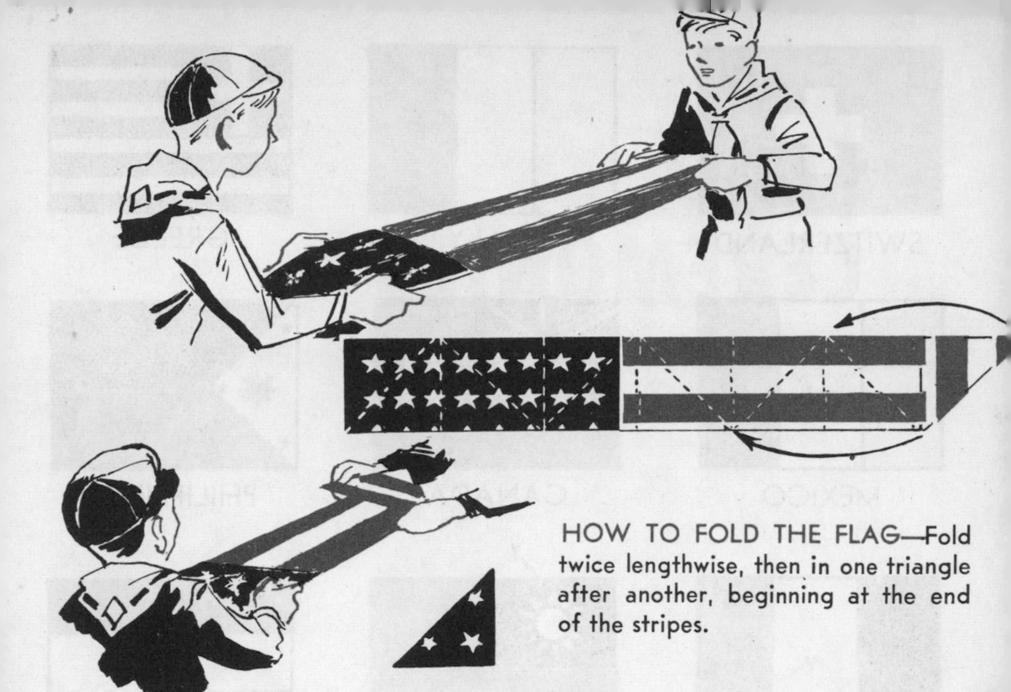

HOW TO FOLD THE FLAG—Fold twice lengthwise, then in one triangle after another, beginning at the end of the stripes.

There are many different kinds of Pack flag ceremonies, but the best ones are the simple ones. You can have a part in one of them. Here are three easy ceremonies for you:

1. Put out all the lights in the room. Have two or three Cub Scouts turn their flashlights on an American Flag in the front of the room. Play the "Star Spangled Banner" on a portable phonograph or have the audience sing the "Star Spangled Banner."
2. Bring the Flag in before the group, then ask them all to stand and repeat the Pledge of Allegiance to the Flag. Leave the Flag in the front of the room.
3. If you have both a Pack flag and an American Flag, two Cub Scouts can carry the flags and two serve as color guards. They come in from a side door and stand in front of the audience as the Cub Scouts all give the salute. Then they walk up the center aisle and out the rear door.

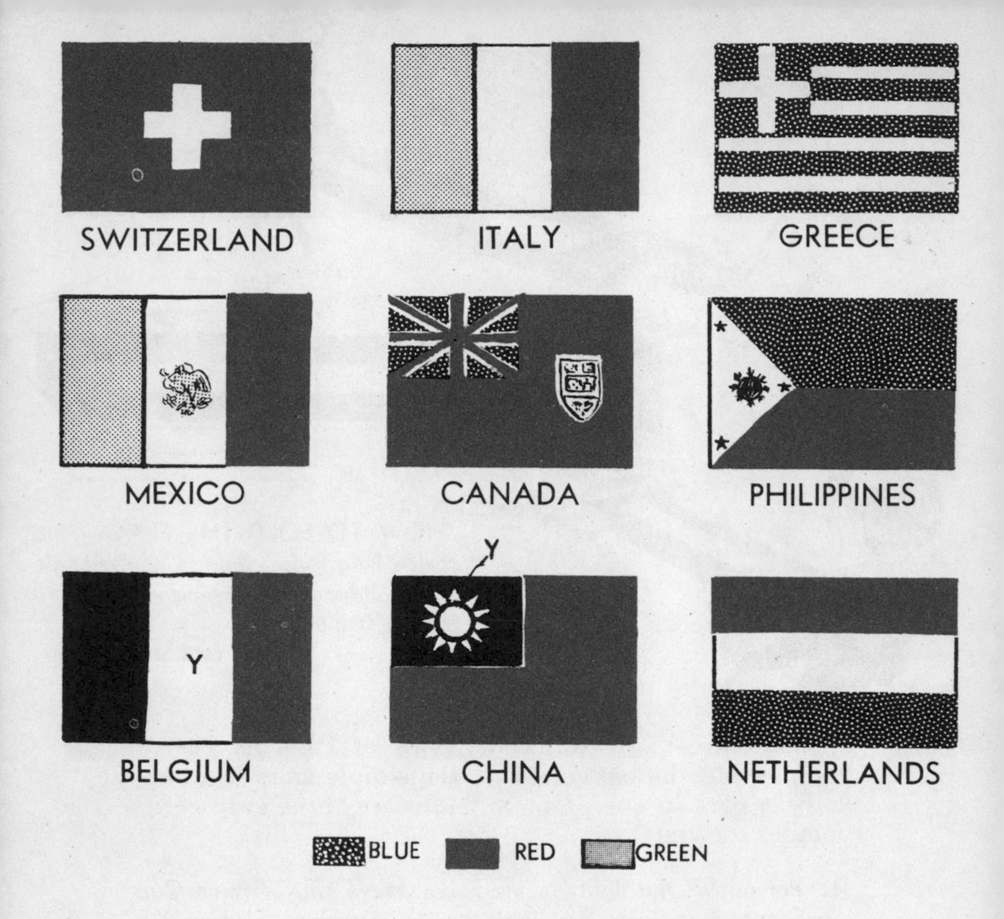

A Cub Scout tries to feel friendly toward all nations, but there may be some that you are especially interested in. It may be because your parents or your grandparents or some of the people living in your neighborhood came from these countries. It may even be because you like the things which people do in these favorite lands of yours.

For this achievement you are asked to draw flags of five nations in which you are interested. Perhaps you will choose countries where you have brother Cub

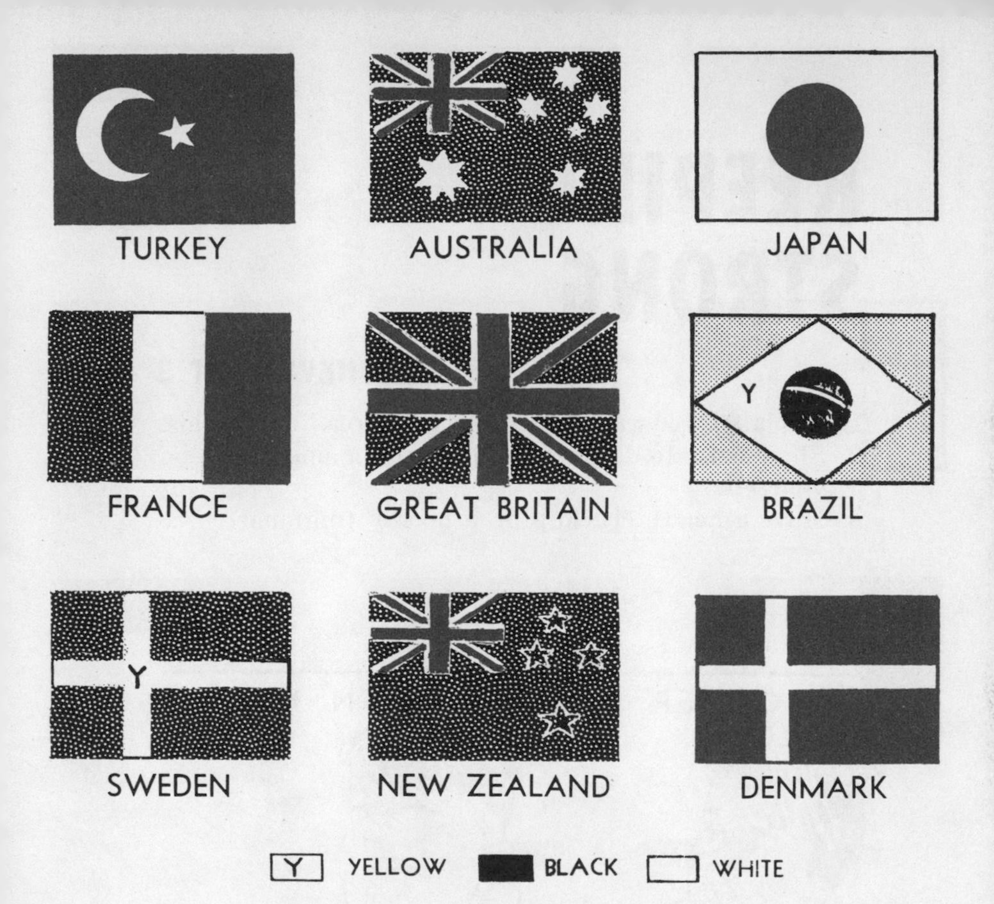

Scouts—countries like Canada, Mexico, Brazil, Great Britain, and France.

When you look at the flag of a country, it tells you something about the people and history of that country. That's why flags are so interesting.

Decide which five nations interest you most. Then ask your teacher or librarian for a book showing the flags of all countries. One place you can find them is in the front of Webster's *New International Dictionary*.

KEEPING STRONG

ACHIEVEMENT 3

1. Explain three ways to prevent the spreading of colds.
2. Show what to do for nosebleed and a small burn on yourself.
3. Have a health checkup by a doctor (optional).

V.R.C. 10-20-57

MOTHER OR DAD SIGN HERE

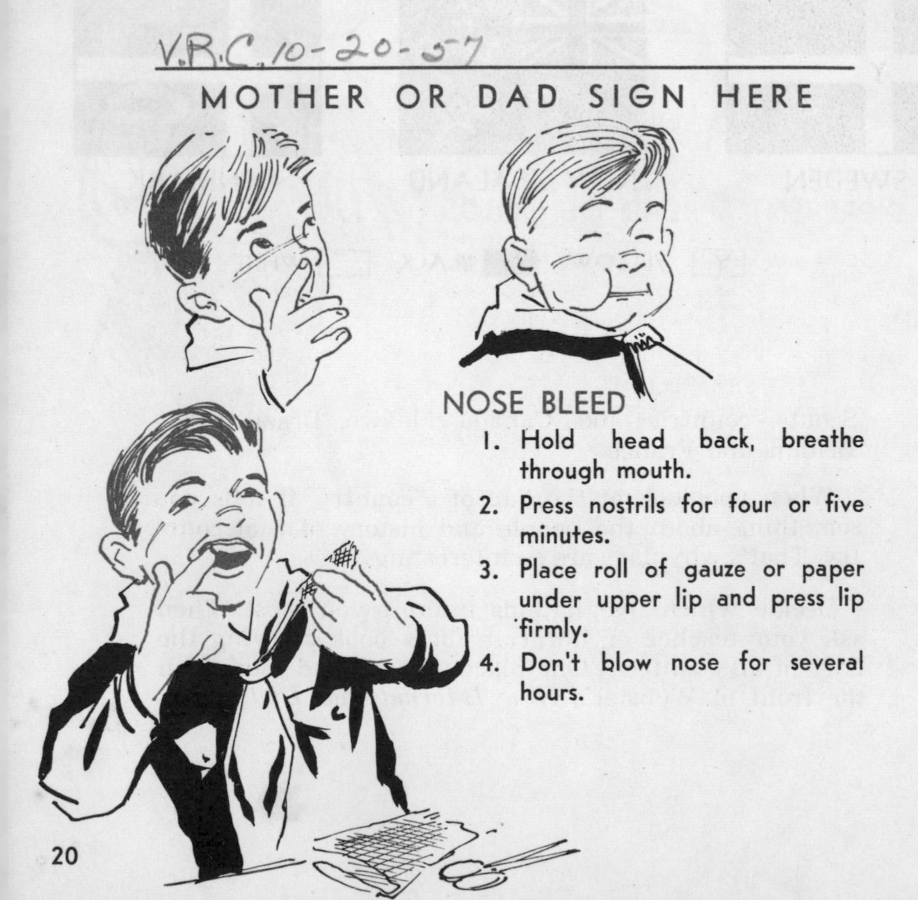

NOSE BLEED

1. Hold head back, breathe through mouth.
2. Press nostrils for four or five minutes.
3. Place roll of gauze or paper under upper lip and press lip firmly.
4. Don't blow nose for several hours.

Each year in Cub Scouting you are having more and more fun. Perhaps it's partly because you are growing stronger.

If you have kept a careful record of your growth through your Wolf and Bear years, check back and see how you compare now with your record for those years. During your Lion year, try to grow stronger so you can be a better Boy Scout when you are eleven.

PREVENT SPREAD OF COLDS

1. If you have a bad cold, stay away from other people as much as possible. STAY HOME AND GET A LOT OF REST IN BED.
2. When you cough or sneeze, turn your head away from others and cover your mouth or nose with a handkerchief.
3. Don't use towels, napkins, food, toys, etc., used by other persons.

NOTE TO PARENTS:

While a health examination by a doctor is not required as part of the Keeping Strong achievement, it is strongly recommended. Every boy should have an annual check-up by a physician. Catch trouble before it becomes serious.

RELIGIOUS SERVICE

ACHIEVEMENT 4

1. Take an active part in your church or synagogue.
2. Do your best to live up to the Cub Scout Promise and the Law of the Pack.

V.R.C. 10-27-57

MOTHER OR DAD SIGN HERE

Your church or synagogue is a friendly place, and you will be spending some time in it all your life. This is your chance to get better acquainted so that you can get the most out of it.

In this achievement (number 4) you will do your part in your church or synagogue. This means you will take part in the religious services and other activities. Perhaps you can help your church or synagogue in a food or clothing collection or by earning and giving money. You may even be able to take on some special good-will activity, such as cutting the lawn or passing out notices.

It won't be long now before you will become a Boy Scout, so you should do a better job than ever of following the Cub Scout Promise and the Law of the Pack. This will help you to be ready to follow the Scout Oath and Scout Law when you are eleven, as you will find out when you begin to work on your Webelos requirements.

TOOLS

ACHIEVEMENT 5

1. Fix up a place for your family woodworking or gardening tools, and take care of them for a period of time agreed upon with your dad.

   OR

   Make or fix something using at least four of the following:

   - Screw driver
   - Saw
   - Hammer
   - Coping Saw
   - Brace and Bit
   - Plane

MOTHER OR DAD SIGN HERE

In your Wolf achievement you learned how to use and take care of your jacknife, and in the Bear achievement you learned how to use a lot of tools.

Now you are getting ready to become a Boy Scout and a Boy Scout does a good turn whenever he can. You can do a good turn for your dad and mother by fixing a place for the family tools and keeping them in order. A good way to do this is to put nails and brackets on the wall by the work bench, so that tools can be hung out of the way. If you make a tool chest, be sure to have a place for each tool, so that they do not scrape together and get dull.

Talk to your dad about this and ask him for help. It's up to you and your dad how long you will keep the tools in order.

For some ideas on things to make with your tools, see the "More Things To Do" section in this book (page 128).

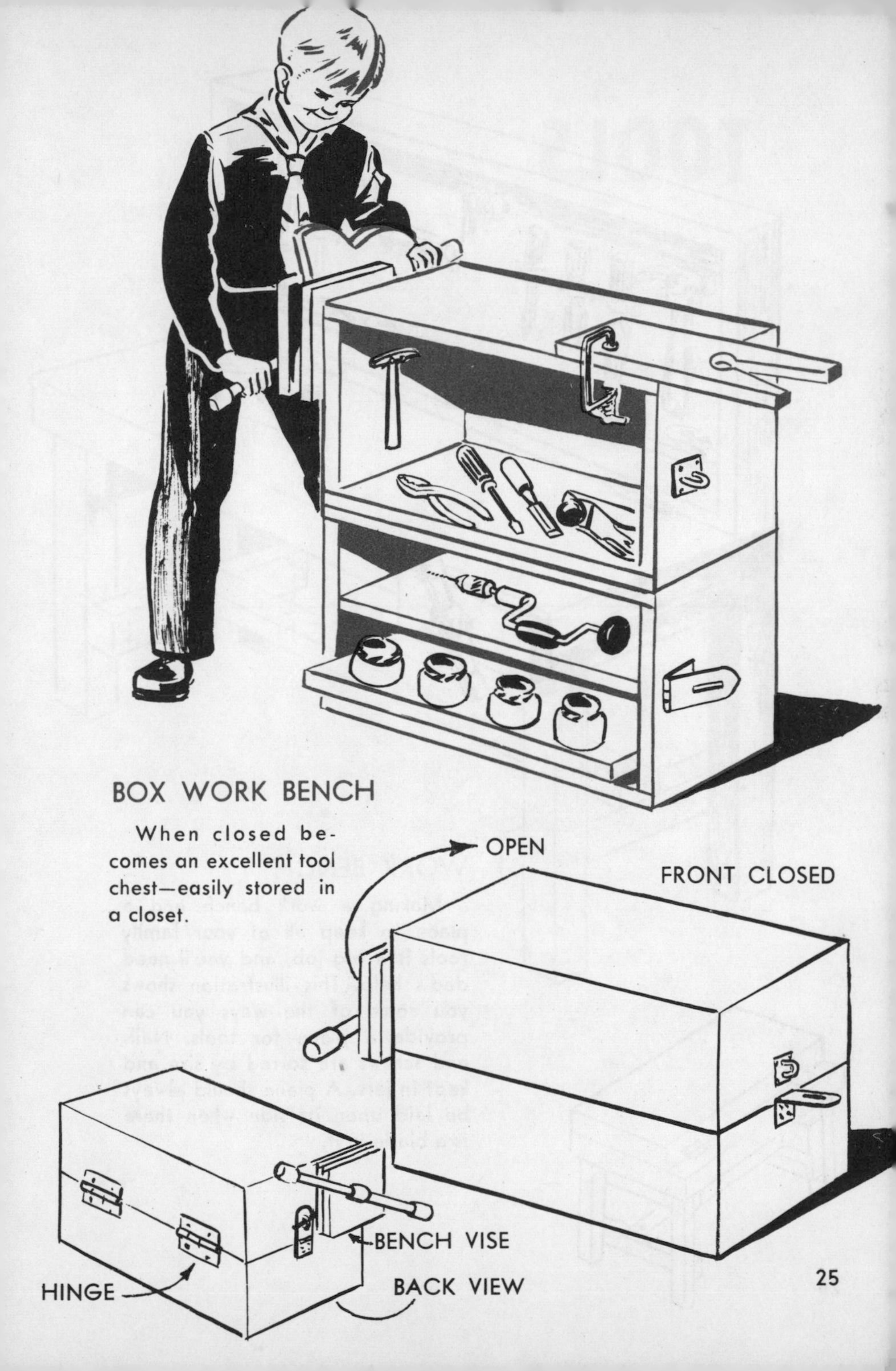

BOX WORK BENCH

When closed becomes an excellent tool chest—easily stored in a closet.

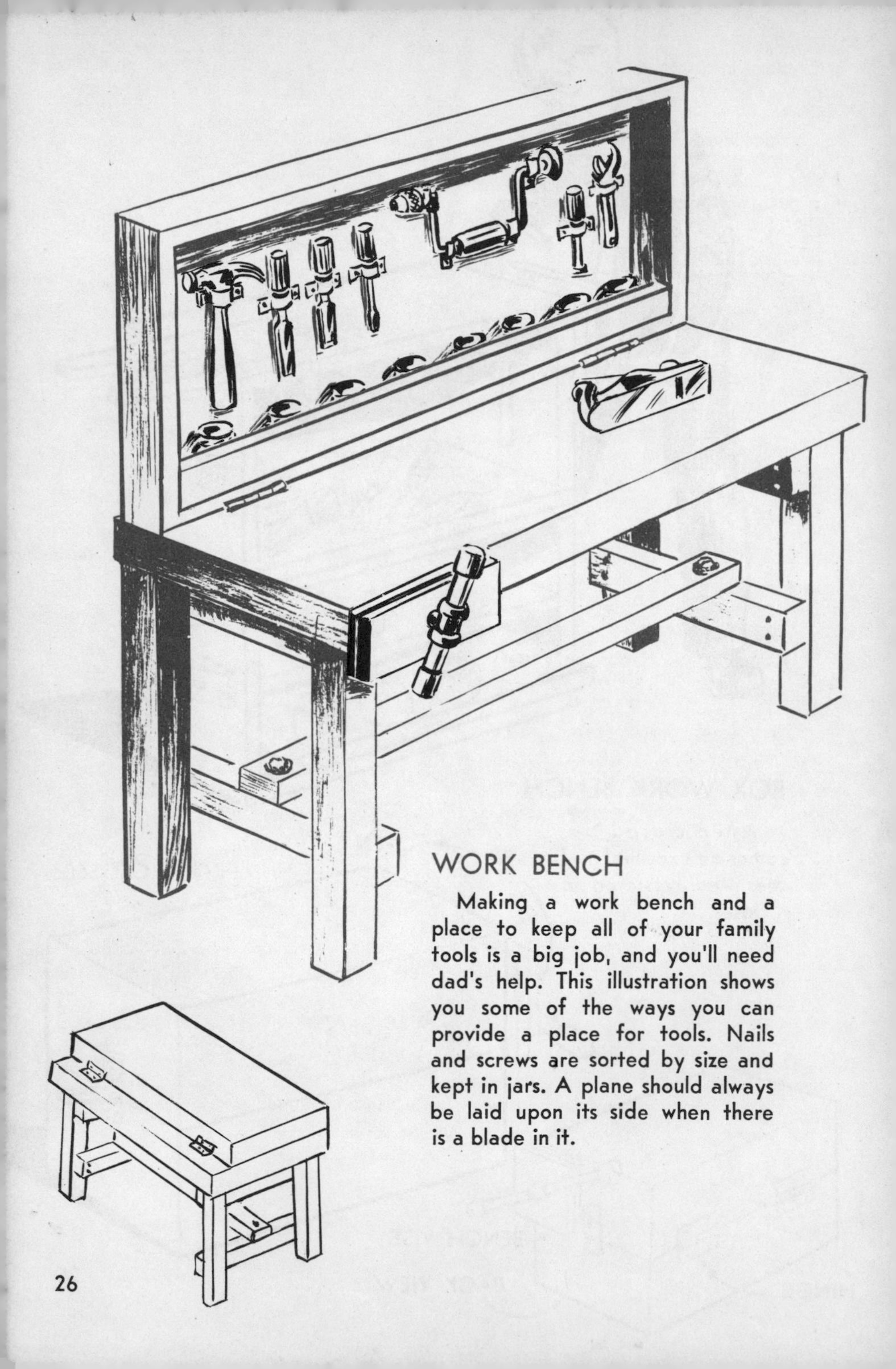

WORK BENCH

Making a work bench and a place to keep all of your family tools is a big job, and you'll need dad's help. This illustration shows you some of the ways you can provide a place for tools. Nails and screws are sorted by size and kept in jars. A plane should always be laid upon its side when there is a blade in it.

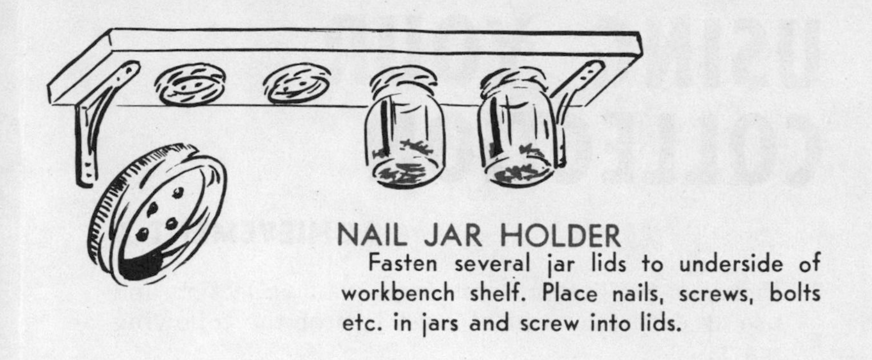

NAIL JAR HOLDER

Fasten several jar lids to underside of workbench shelf. Place nails, screws, bolts etc. in jars and screw into lids.

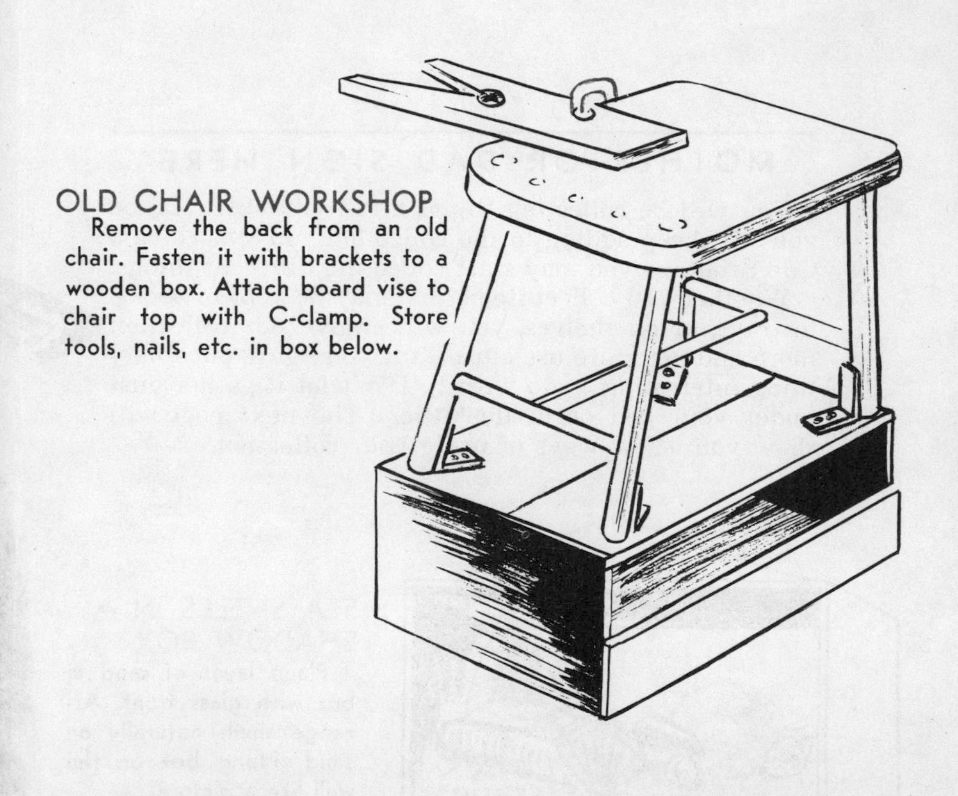

OLD CHAIR WORKSHOP

Remove the back from an old chair. Fasten it with brackets to a wooden box. Attach board vise to chair top with C-clamp. Store tools, nails, etc. in box below.

USING YOUR COLLECTION

ACHIEVEMENT 6

1. Pick out the better items from your collection and use as decorations in at least two of the following ways:

Frame them	A screen
Put in a shadow box	A lamp
Table top cover	A wall plaque

VRC - 1-1-58

MOTHER OR DAD SIGN HERE

You will be collecting things all of your life. Maybe you will keep adding to the collection you started as a Cub Scout, or you may start collecting different things.

Whether you collect items that may be kept in books, in trays, or on shelves, you will enjoy your collection more and get more use out of it if you figure out something interesting to do with it. Don't let it gather dust under your bed or in the attic. The next page will show you a few ways of using your collection.

SEA SHELLS IN A SHADOW BOX

Place layer of sand in box with glass front. Arrange shells naturally on sand. Hang box on the wall like a picture.

ARRANGE ROCKS
LIKE A MOUNTAIN

LEAVES ON A LAMP

STAMPS ON CLOTH

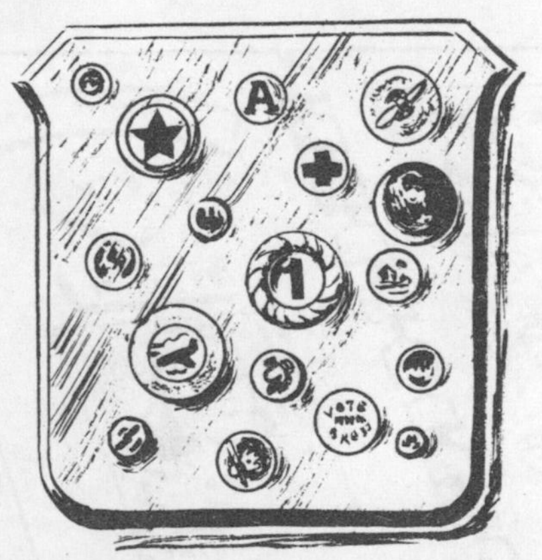

BUTTONS ON A PLAQUE

SCREEN OF
AIRPLANE VIEWS

LOG BOOK

ACHIEVEMENT 7

1. Make a log book record (with at least 25 pages) of your Cub Scout activities.
   You may include snapshots, programs, party favors, souvenirs, sketches, autographs, announcements, newspaper stories of Den and Pack activities, as well as maps, booklets and stories of your family trips.

VRC - 1-4-58

MOTHER OR DAD SIGN HERE

It won't be long now! In a few more months you will be eleven years old and ready to be a Boy Scout.

For your Lion rank why don't you make your log

Why not make a memory book of all the things you have done as a Cub Scout? You'll have fun looking through it in many years to come.

book a Cub Scout activities book? You can take pictures of your Den doings, of your Den backyard, and of the things you did on your picnic or your family trips. You can include drawings of your favorite games, a sketch of your Den doodle, or you can cut out magazine pictures which remind you of some of the places you have been.

You can collect pictures of Boy Scouts from papers and magazines. You can cut pictures out of BOYS' LIFE Magazine, which shows things Boy Scouts do. There will be pictures about camping, tying knots, cooking, chopping wood, boating, etc. These are the things you will be doing when you become a Scout, and this is a good time to learn all about them by making a Boy Scout hobby book.

Why not make a memory book of all the things you have done as a Cub Scout? You'll have fun looking through it in many years to come.

Be prepared! Begin a scrapbook about things Boy Scouts do. Get a head start before you're eleven.

Be Prepared! Begin a scrapbook about things Boy Scouts do. Get a head start before you're eleven.

USING ROPE

ACHIEVEMENT 8

Do the following:

1. Make a tetherball game.
2. Improvise rope handles for a storage chest, clothes basket, or a gate.
3. Make a set of rope quoits.
4. Make a swing or trapeze.

Virginia Chesson 1-6-57

MOTHER OR DAD SIGN HERE

Did you ever play with a piece of rope and wish you could make something with it besides a lasso? Well, here are four ways of using rope that will be fun.

The trapeze or swing can be set up in your backyard or hung from a strong beam in the garage. Better get

dad's okay before you do this one. Have him test the ropes and the knots you've tied. If it will hold him it will stand up under the hard workout you and your buddy will give it.

OUTDOOR SAFETY

ACHIEVEMENT 9

1. Know the rules for water safety.
2. Practice the rules of boat safety.
3. Practice the rules of outdoor fire safety.

MOTHER OR DAD SIGN HERE

A lake is a fine place to have a lot of fun—*if* it is a lake you know, and *if* you understand a few water safety rules. It's good to learn them now as a Lion Cub Scout because you will be doing a lot of swimming as a Boy Scout.

There's something in this achievement for you and your dad to do together.

WATER SAFETY RULES

1. Swim only when a good adult swimmer is on watch.
2. Always swim with a buddy and keep him in sight all the time.
3. Don't swim out in water over your shoulders unless you are a very good swimmer.
4. Avoid stomach cramps. Wait two hours after eating before you swim.
5. Never dive into strange water. Find out first what is below the surface.
6. Rowboats and canoes are not toys. Don't rock or play around in them. If craft overturns or swamps, *hang on to it until help comes.*

FAMILY FUN

ACHIEVEMENT 10

1. Make a family record book or album, including pictures of relatives, birth dates, etc.

OR

2. Go on a family trip such as a visit to a museum, a creamery, an airport or other place of interest.

If there is a good reason why you cannot do this, arrange with your Cubmaster to do something as nearly like it as you can.

V. R. C. 10-20-57

MOTHER OR DAD SIGN HERE

Ask your mother and dad if they have some old pictures taken when they were very young. You will have fun looking at the funny clothes worn back when they were small. They will have some pictures of you when you were small, too, and you will probably even think they are funny, especially if they have some baby pictures of you. It would be too bad for these old pictures to get lost, so get your mother and dad to help you gather them together and put them into an album. It will be sort of a history of your family.

If you don't want to make an album, you and your family can take a trip to some interesting place. If there is a zoo near you, it would be a lot of fun to go there, or to an airport or a museum. An ice cream factory is fun to visit, and you may even get a free sample.

TRAVEL FROM HOME

ACHIEVEMENT 11

Did you ever watch a train go through your town, or an airplane fly over? Didn't you ever wonder where they were going? Wouldn't it be interesting to find out?

Find out about the railroads, buses, and airplanes that go through or over your town. Then try to plan a trip going to some of the places they might take you. You will be surprised to find how much quicker you can go by plane than by train, and you will know after this when you see a plane go over your house where it is going and where it came from. Some day you'll be flying, and it's good to find out about it now.

1. Find out some of the railroads, bus lines, or airlines that pass through your city or town or near it, and discover some of the places they go.
2. Try your hand at using timetables by planning a trip from your home or nearest station to a city in another state by railroad, bus or airline.
3. Find out what it costs per mile to travel by bus, railroad or plane.

VRC – 11-29-57

MOTHER OR DAD SIGN HERE

STORY TELLING

ACHIEVEMENT 12

1. Tell a story to your Den using puppets.
2. Ask your parents or librarian to help you make a list of books. Read two of them.
3. Learn how to fix the cover or binding of a book and make a paper cover.

____

MOTHER OR DAD SIGN HERE

What would you like to know? Why the wind blows? Why the ocean is salty? Why you see lightning before you hear the thunder? Why a cat's eyes gleam in the dark?

Books give you the answers. That's why it's fun to read. Ask your teacher or librarian to show you how to use special books like an encyclopedia, in which you can look up answers to questions that you are wondering about. But every book you read will answer some questions, so read and read some more. It's lots of fun.

It's fun to tell a story with puppets! While it takes a little more time to do it this way, you'll think it's worth the trouble when some one says, "Gee, that was swell!"

Pick out a story you like. Read it through and then write down a bare outline of what you want to say. To tell a good story you must know the names of the

characters, what they do and, more or less, what they say. A good beginning and a good ending should be learned. Once you get started telling your story you'll have no trouble. Read your story over and over, and then tell it to mother or dad for practice. You'll be surprised at how easy it is for you to do.

You needn't make all of the characters in the story—just one or two main ones that you want to tell about.

BOOK COVER

Use a heavy sheet of paper about twice the width of the book. Fold top and bottom inward to match height of book. Now fold each end inward, and tuck book covers into flaps formed, as shown.

A R R O W

Look through the list of electives, choose the ones you want to do, then start on the one you like best.

E L E C T I V E S

1. **SIGNALS**
2. **PUPPETS AND THINGS**
3. **CRAFTSMAN**
4. **RADIO**
5. **ELECTRICIAN**
6. **BOAT BUILDER**
7. **SKY OBSERVER**
8. **THINGS THAT GO**
9. **MECHANIC**
10. **PARTY GIVER**
11. **INDIAN DANCER**
12. **MUSICIAN**
13. **MASKS**
14. **PHOTOS**
15. **NATURE**
16. **DOGS**
17. **LANDSCAPER**
18. **SOIL AND WATER CONSERVATION**
19. **OUTDOOR CHEF**
20. **SHELTERS**
21. **SWIMMING**
22. **SAFETY SERVICE**
23. **SPORTS**

P O I N T S

The following pages are packed with interesting things to do. The pictures do not try to tell you how to do everything. That would be impossible in a single book like this. But you will find a great many ideas out of the hundreds of things you can make and do to earn Arrow Points. If you like, you may go back to your Wolf and Bear Cub Scout books and do some of the electives described in them (if you have not already done them) to earn Lion Arrow Points.

Now—pick the thing you like best, and get ready for some real fun.

If you are 10½ years old, you may begin to work for your Webelos badge.

However, if you are not old enough for that, you'll find plenty to do earning your Lion Arrow Points.

Look through the electives. Notice all the brand new things to do?

You don't have to do all of the things listed under an elective to earn a credit. Each time you do any one of them you earn a credit. When you show mother or dad you can do the requirement, they will sign their initials and write the date on the line provided for signing in

each elective. In the circle they will write the number of the thing you did. Like this:

MOTHER'S OR DAD'S INITIALS AND DATE FOR EACH CREDIT

(6) G.R.H. 10/15/54 ( ) ______

Each time you do one of the things suggested, you will receive an Arrow Point credit. In the box score on this page write in the numbers of the electives you earn. When you have ten credits, you will receive your Gold Arrow Point. Wear it under your Lion badge. For each additional ten credits, you will receive a Silver Arrow Point. There is no limit to the number of Silver Arrow Points you may earn.

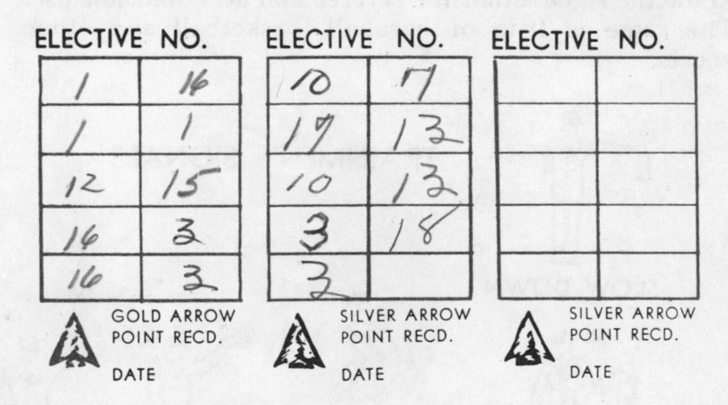

BOX SCORE OF MY ELECTIVE CREDITS

ELECTIVE NO.		ELECTIVE NO.		ELECTIVE NO.	
1	16	10	17		
1	1	17	13		
12	15	10	13		
16	3	3	18		
16	3	3			

GOLD ARROW POINT RECD.
DATE

SILVER ARROW POINT RECD.
DATE

SILVER ARROW POINT RECD.
DATE

SIGNALS

ELECTIVE 1

You can do each one of the following only once for credit in the Lion book:

1. Know and show the signs used by broadcasting studios.
2. Know and show the signs used by referees in football, baseball, or basketball.
3. Know the signs used by trainmen or air field signals.

MOTHER'S OR DAD'S INITIALS AND DATE FOR EACH CREDIT

1 V.R.C. 11-2-57
2 V.R.C. 11-2-57
3 V.R.C. 11-2-57

It's a lot more fun to watch a big football game if you know the signals that the referee and other officials use. The same is true of baseball, basketball and other sports.

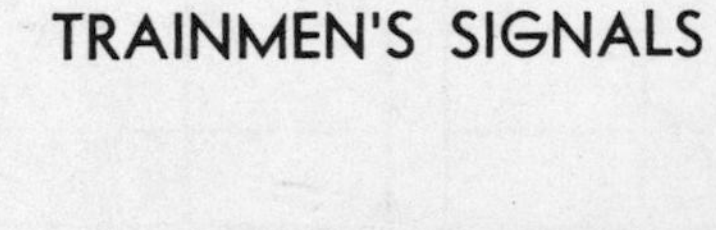

Airmen, trainmen and broadcasters have their signals, too. Learn them and make your next railroad or broadcasting skit sound real.

SIGNALS IN THE BROADCASTING STUDIO

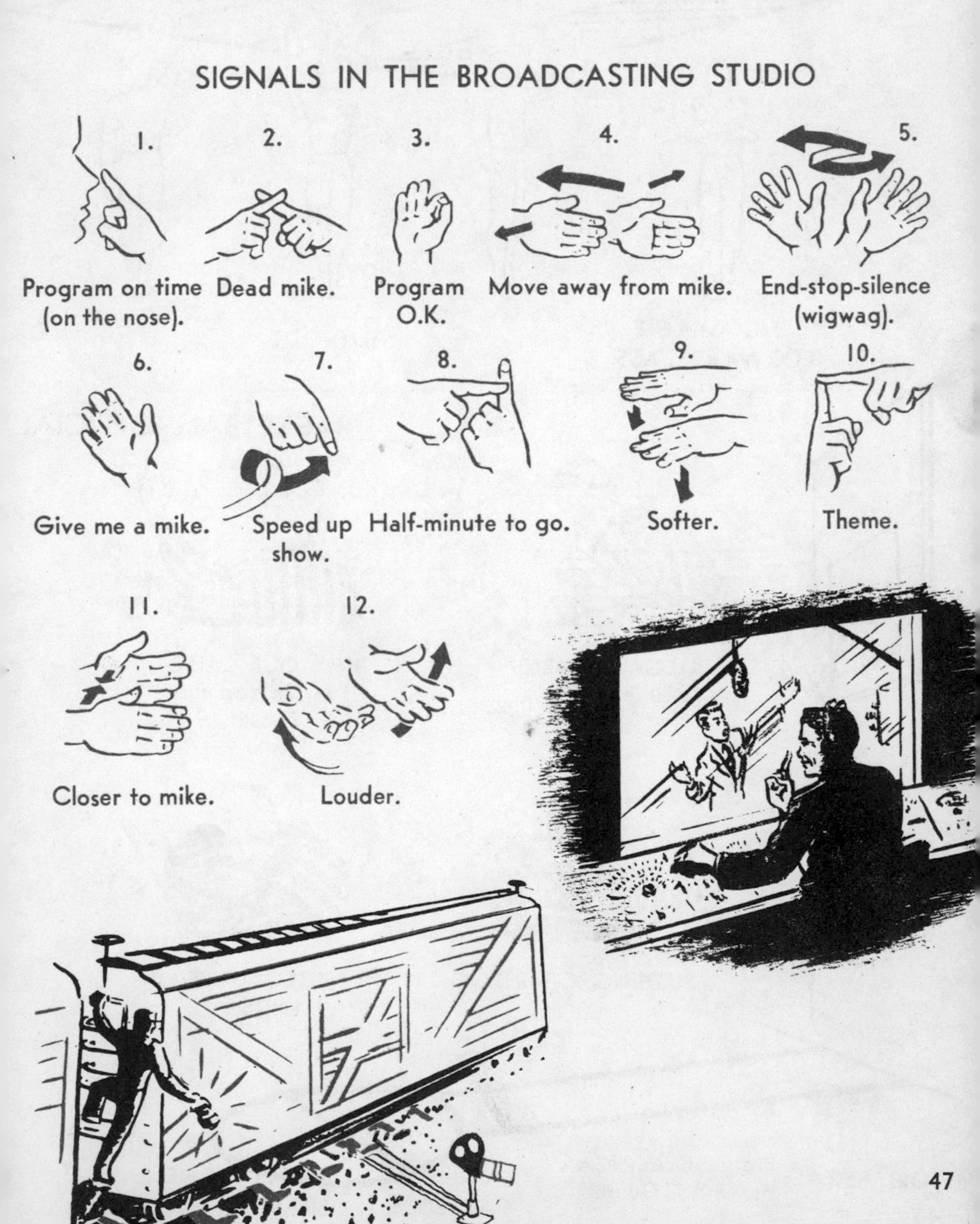

FOOTBALL OFFICIAL CODE SIGNALS
FIRST DOWN
BALL DOWN
INCOMPLETE
FORWARD PASS
TIME OUT
BASKETBALL OFFICIAL
ILLEGAL DRIBBLE
Patting Motion
TIME OUT CALLED
A. To stop clock
B. Substitute may
enter
PUSHING, CHARGING
ILLEGAL USE OF
HANDS
From Official NCAA
Basketball Guide

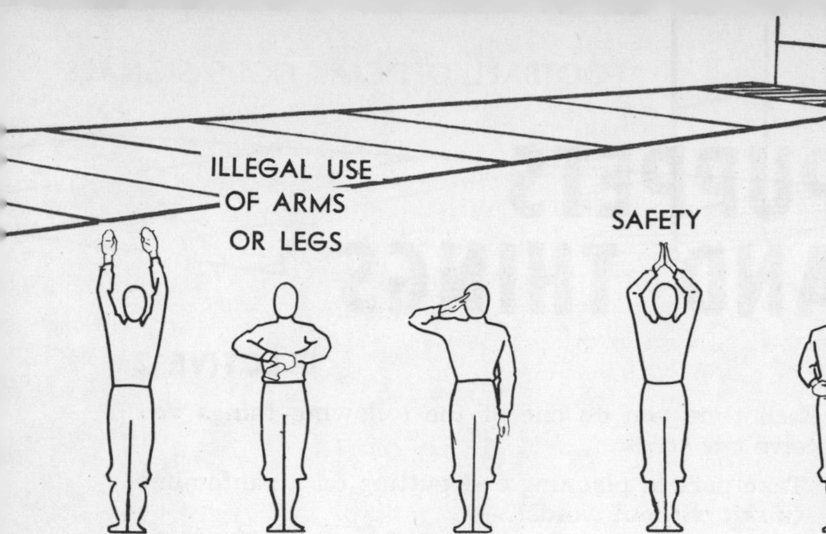
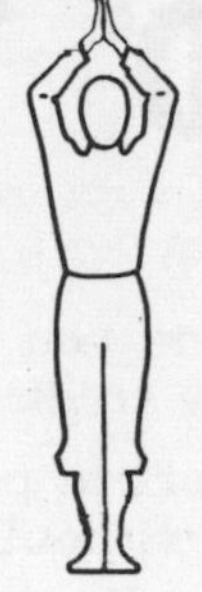

ILLEGAL USE OF ARMS OR LEGS

SAFETY

TOUCHDOWN OR FIELD GOAL

UNNECESSARY ROUGHNESS

OFF SIDE

CODE SIGNALS

TIME OUT WITH FOUL

TECHNICAL FOUL

HOLDING

TO POINT OUT OFFENDER

A. SCORE COUNTS
B. NO FREE THROWS

CANCEL SCORE

HELD BALL

VIOLATION OUT OF BOUNDS

PUPPETS AND THINGS

ELECTIVE 2

Each time you do one of the following things you receive *one credit.*

1. Take part in planning and putting on a pantomime (a skit without words).
2. Lead the Den in a game of charades.
3. Make some hand or string puppets.
4. Make a puppet theater.
5. Help make a large circus animal.

MOTHER'S OR DAD'S INITIALS AND DATE FOR EACH CREDIT

② VRC-5/21/58

Puppets are more fun than ever when you make string puppets. You make them act by pulling strings which are fastened to them. They are not hard to make, either.

String puppets take a special kind of puppet theater because it will have to be big enough so that you can reach down from above it as you pull the strings.

If you take part in a Den stunt or circus, you will be able to make some big animals. You don't have to be an artist. Just follow some of the hints which you will find on the next page or two.

CIRCUS ANIMALS ARE FUN

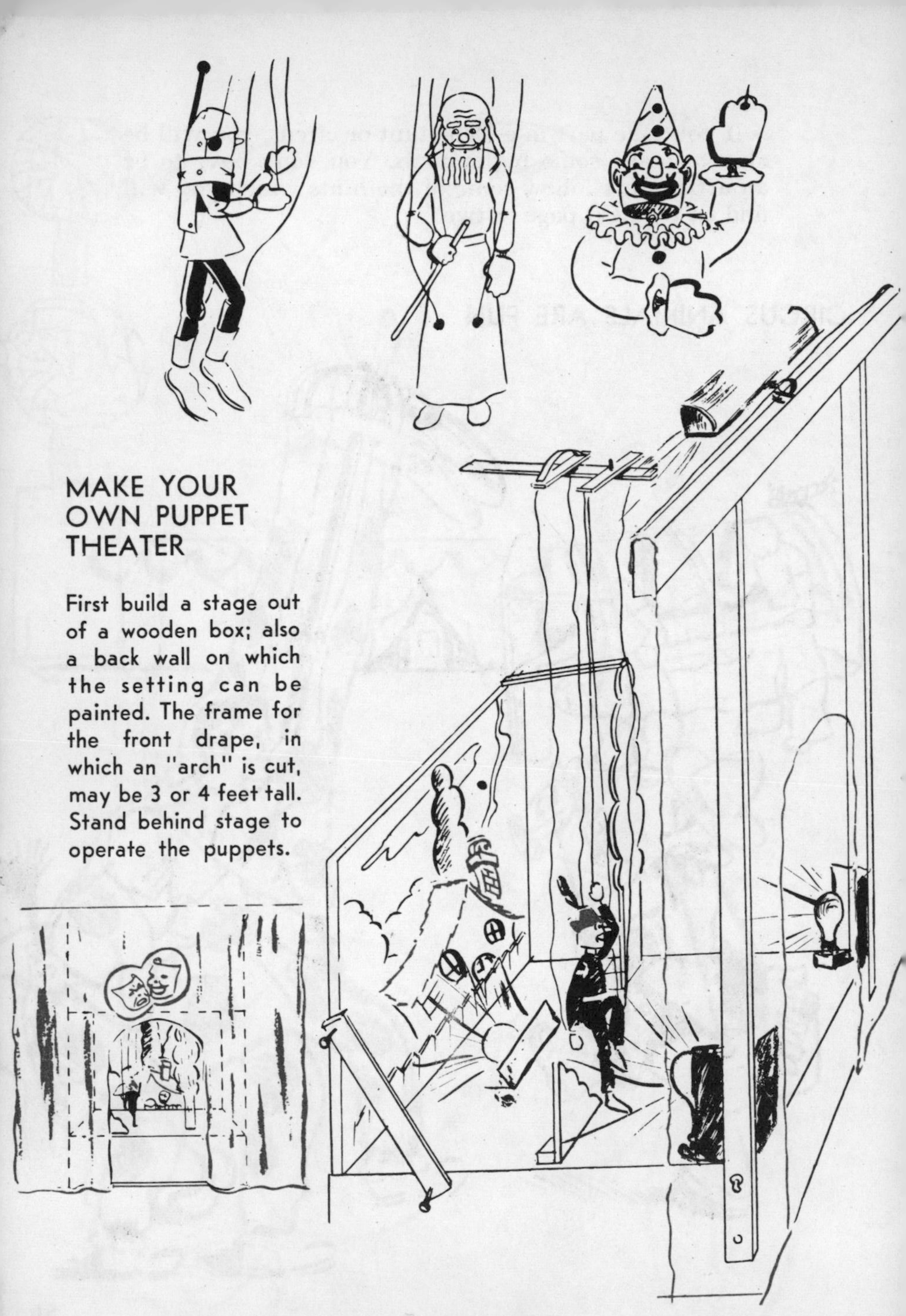

MAKE YOUR OWN PUPPET THEATER

First build a stage out of a wooden box; also a back wall on which the setting can be painted. The frame for the front drape, in which an "arch" is cut, may be 3 or 4 feet tall. Stand behind stage to operate the puppets.

CRAFTSMAN

ELECTIVE 3

For each thing you make you receive *one credit.*

1. Make something useful for the home.
2. Make a neckerchief slide.

MOTHER'S OR DAD'S INITIALS AND DATE FOR EACH CREDIT

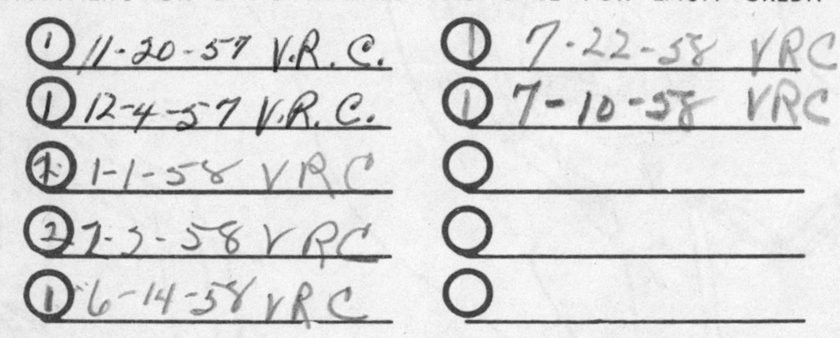

If you have a Cub Scout uniform, you have used neckerchief slides. You can use them when you become a Scout, too. There are many different kinds of neckerchief slides to make, as you can see, and it's more fun to make your own.

Maybe you'd like to make a neckerchief slide for your Den Chief or your Cubmaster, too. You could even make one for the Scoutmaster of the Troop you will join.

NECKERCHIEF SLIDES

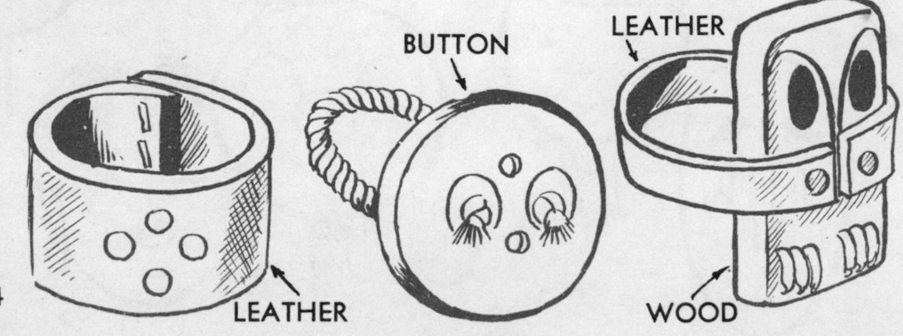

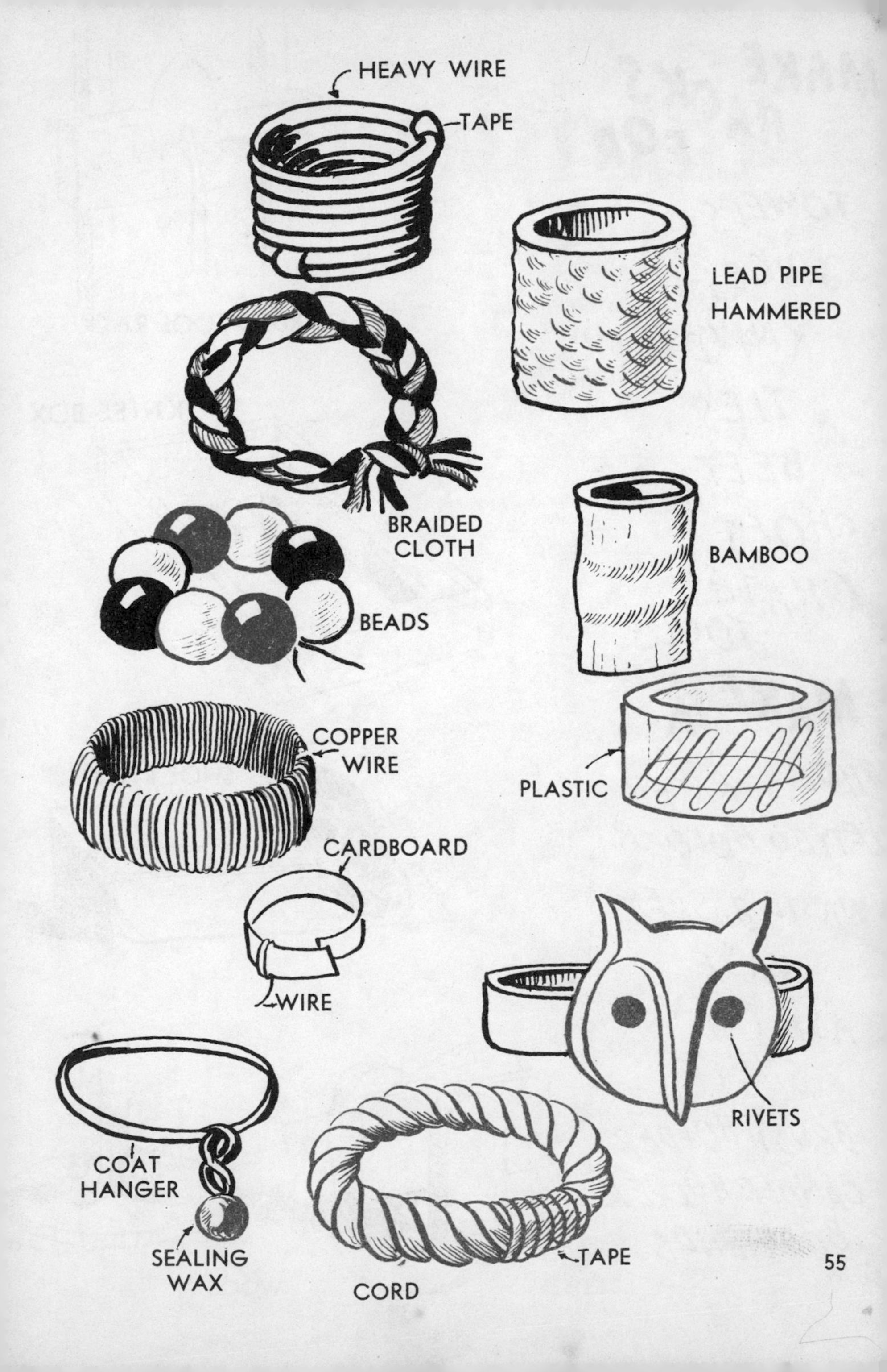
HEAVY WIRE
TAPE
LEAD PIPE HAMMERED
BRAIDED CLOTH
BAMBOO
BEADS
COPPER WIRE
PLASTIC
CARDBOARD
WIRE
RIVETS
COAT HANGER
SEALING WAX
TAPE
CORD

MAKE RACKS FOR

TOWELS
SPICES
KNIVES
TIES
BELTS
SHOES
HATS
TOOLS

MAKE A

SHOE SCRAPER
LETTER HOLDER
WASTE BASKET
VASE
ASH TRAY
SHELF
BRUSH HOLDER
CANDLE HOLDER
BOOK ENDS

GARDEN TOOL RACK

KNIFE BOX

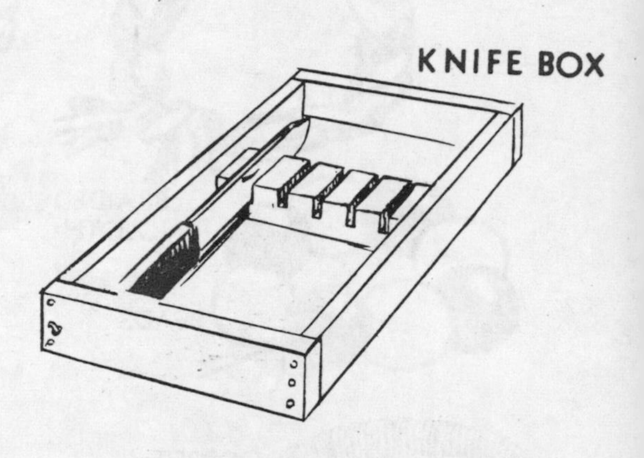

SHOE RACK

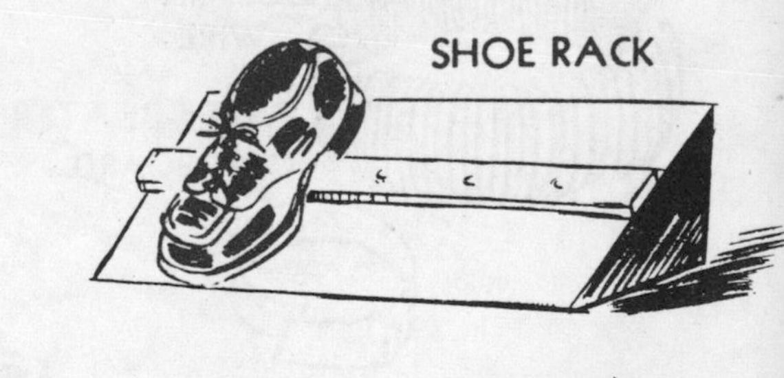

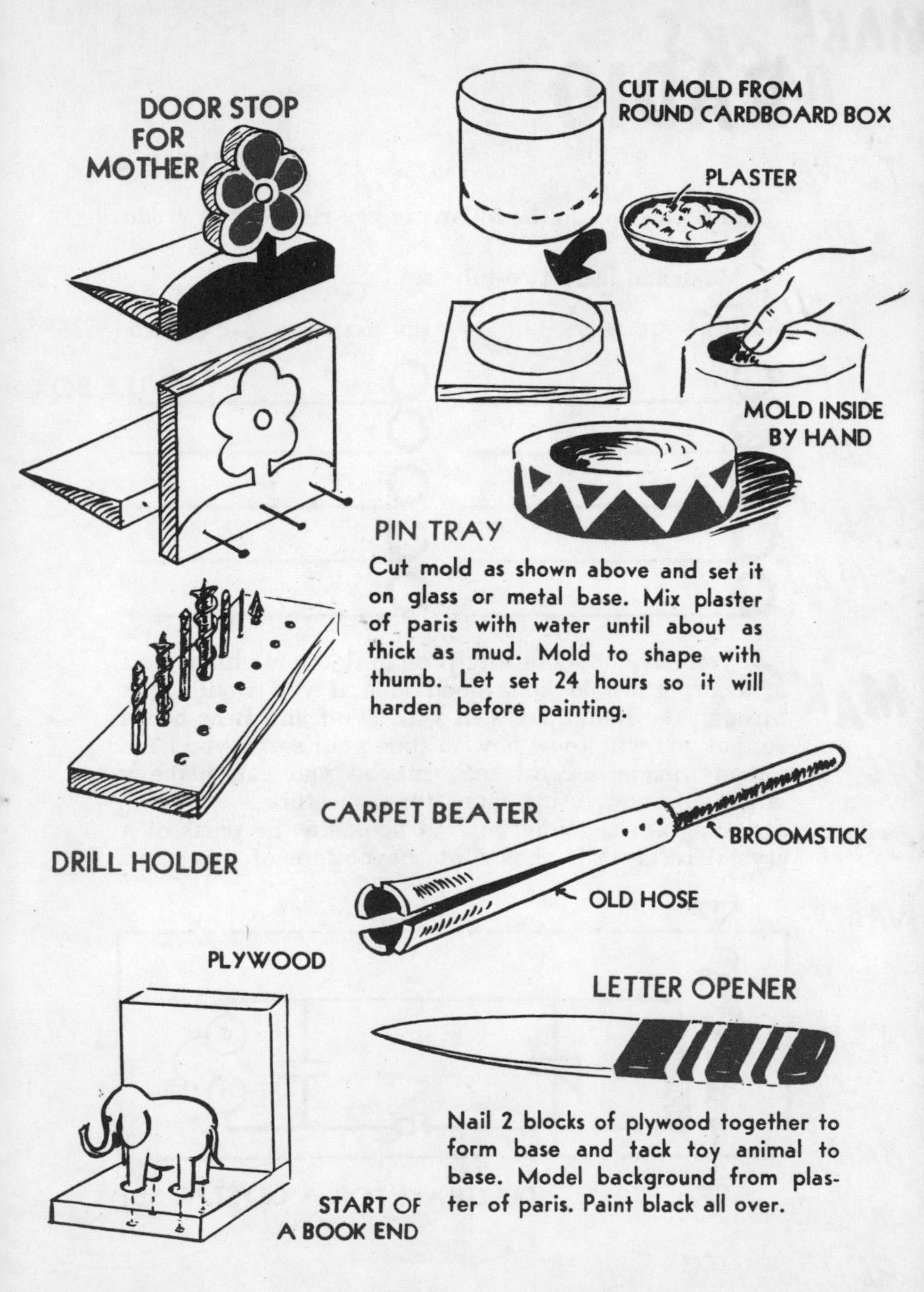

Cut mold as shown above and set it on glass or metal base. Mix plaster of paris with water until about as thick as mud. Mold to shape with thumb. Let set 24 hours so it will harden before painting.

Nail 2 blocks of plywood together to form base and tack toy animal to base. Model background from plaster of paris. Paint black all over.

RADIO

ELECTIVE 4

Each time you do the following you receive *one credit.*

1. Make and use a two-tube set.

MOTHER'S OR DAD'S INITIALS AND DATE FOR EACH CREDIT

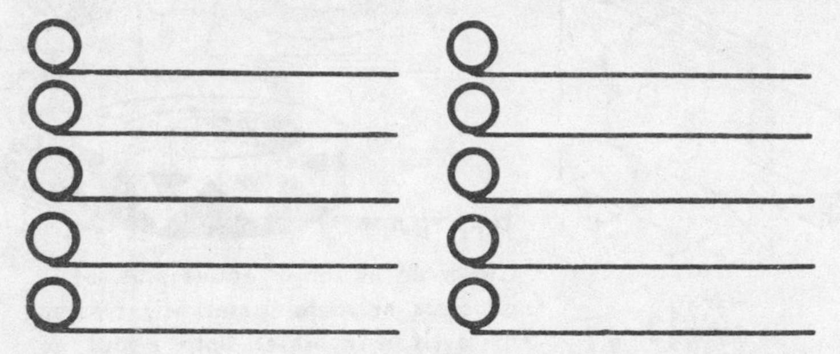

If you have not done anything in Radio in either Wolf or Bear, it would be a good idea if you would look through the Radio pages in your Wolf and Bear books so that you will know how to start your set. If you have already made several sets, maybe you can make a larger one now, using more than one tube.

A diagram showing how to hook up the parts of a crystal receiver is shown at the bottom of this page.

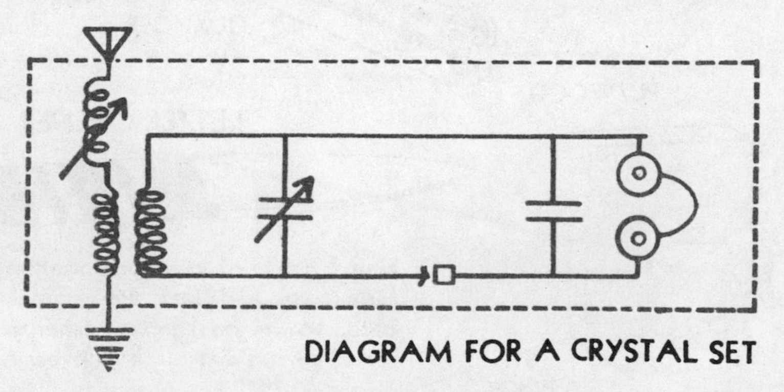

DIAGRAM FOR A CRYSTAL SET

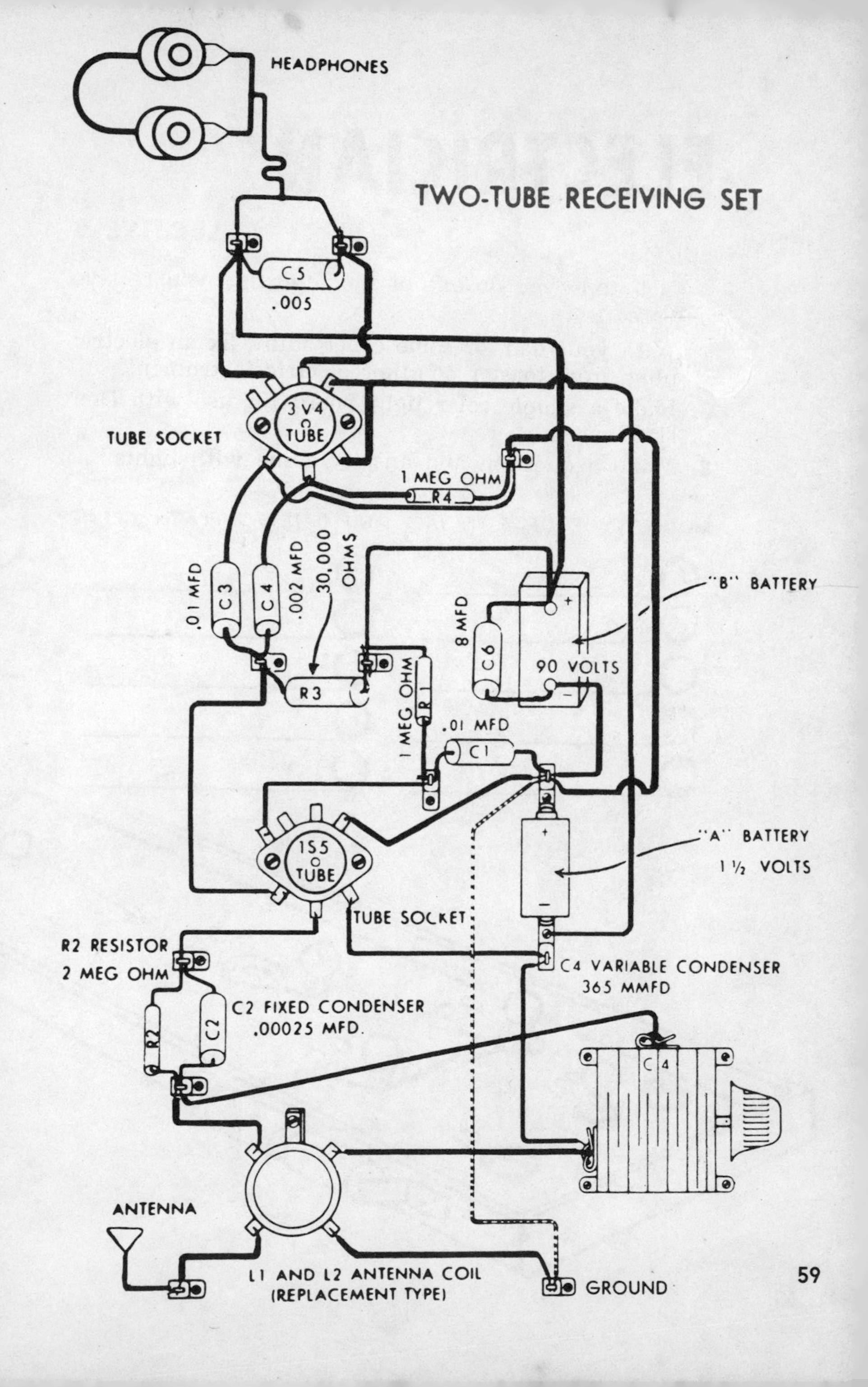
HEADPHONES
TWO-TUBE RECEIVING SET
C5
.005
3V4
TUBE
TUBE SOCKET
1 MEG OHM
R4
"B" BATTERY
C3
.01 MFD
C4
.002 MFD
30,000
OHMS
8 MFD
C6
+
90 VOLTS
−
R3
R1
1 MEG OHM
.01 MFD
C1
1S5
TUBE
+
"A" BATTERY
1 ½ VOLTS
−
TUBE SOCKET
R2 RESISTOR
2 MEG OHM
C4 VARIABLE CONDENSER
365 MMFD
R2
C2
C2 FIXED CONDENSER
.00025 MFD.
C4
ANTENNA
L1 AND L2 ANTENNA COIL
(REPLACEMENT TYPE)
GROUND

ELECTRICIAN

ELECTIVE 5

Each time you do one of the following you receive *one credit.*

1. With your dad, or some other adult, fix an electric plug, iron, toaster or other electric instrument.
2. Make a simple color light board for use with Den skits.
3. Make a question and answer game with lights.

MOTHER'S OR DAD'S INITIALS AND DATE FOR EACH CREDIT

(1) 2-23-58 CEC

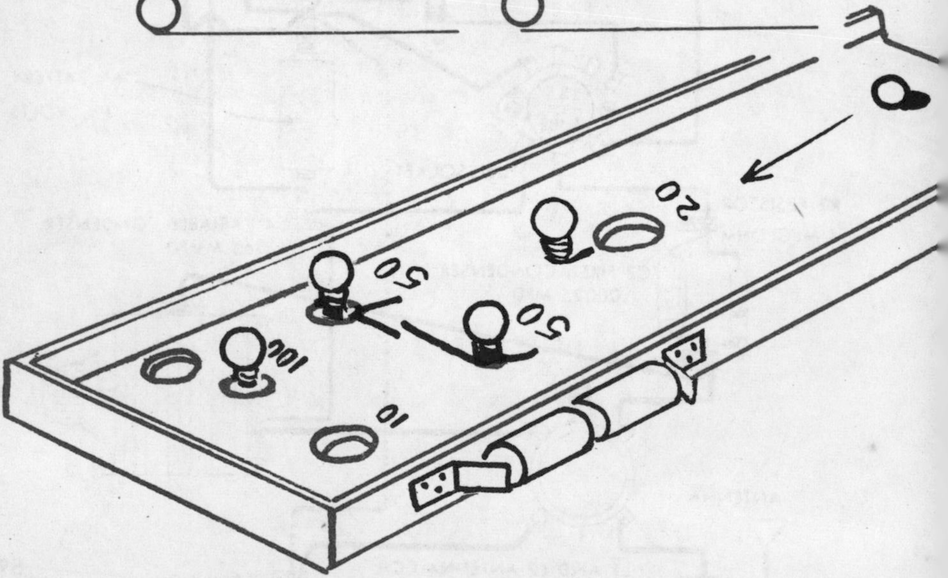

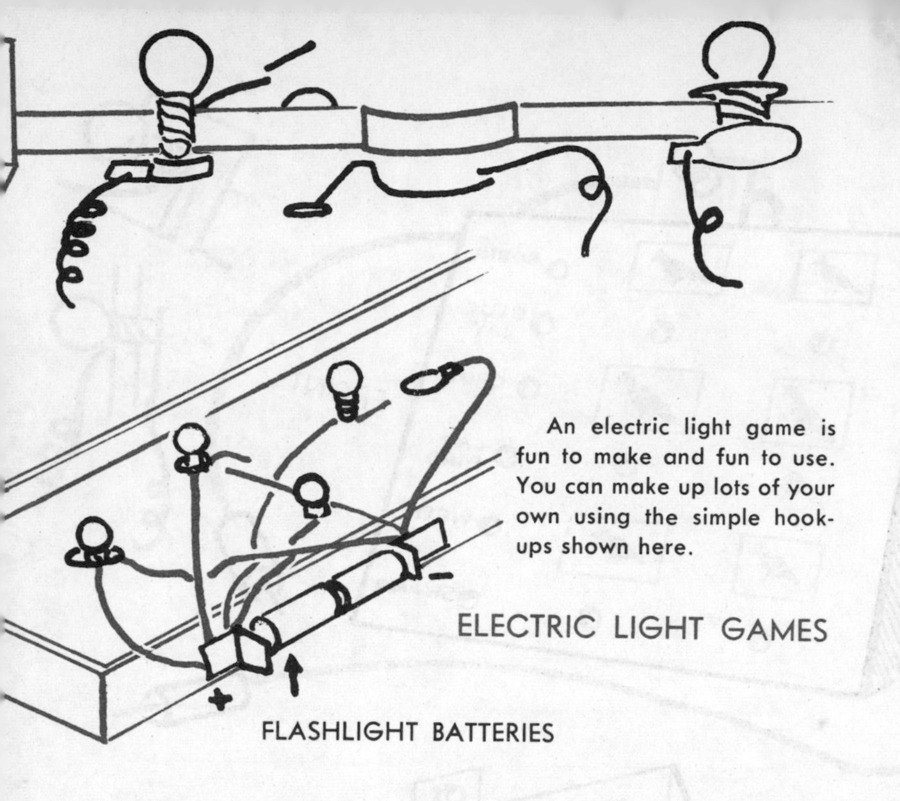

An electric light game is fun to make and fun to use. You can make up lots of your own using the simple hook-ups shown here.

ELECTRIC LIGHT GAMES

It would be a good idea to look back through your Wolf and Bear books if you like electricity, because there are probably some things there you have not yet done.

Did your doorbell ever get out of order? Sometimes when it happens it's just because the connections come loose or the wires corrode. If you know how to wire a doorbell, you will probably know how to fix it. If you wish, you may just mount a doorbell on a piece of wood in order to learn how to wire it. Get your dad to work with you on this.

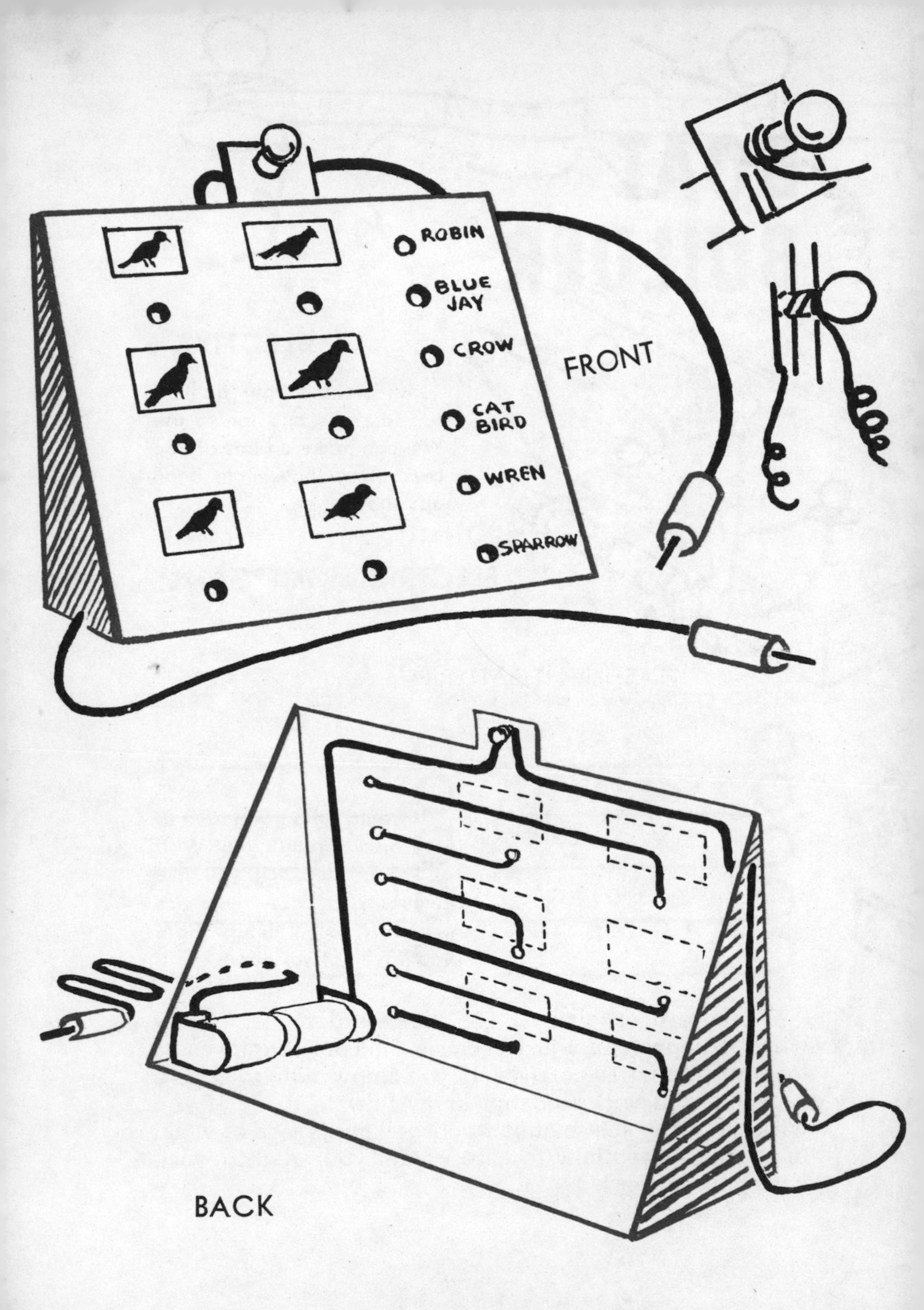
ROBIN
BLUE JAY
CROW
CAT BIRD
WREN
SPARROW
FRONT
BACK

BOAT BUILDER

ELECTIVE 6

Each time you do one of the following things you receive *one credit.*

1. Help your dad or some other adult repair a real boat or canoe.
2. Help your dad or some other adult rig and sail a real boat.
3. With your dad or some other adult build a real raft.
4. Help your dad or some other adult repair a boat dock.

MOTHER'S OR DAD'S INITIALS AND DATE FOR EACH CREDIT

Sailing is great sport. Help your dad or some other adult rig and sail a real boat. If you live near a pond or lake, perhaps you have a boat dock or need to build one. You can earn credit by helping your dad or some other adult fix up his dock.

If your dad is a hunter or fisherman he probably has a boat or canoe which needs repair. Learn how by helping him or some other adult fix his boat or canoe, and earn credit toward your Arrow Point by doing so.

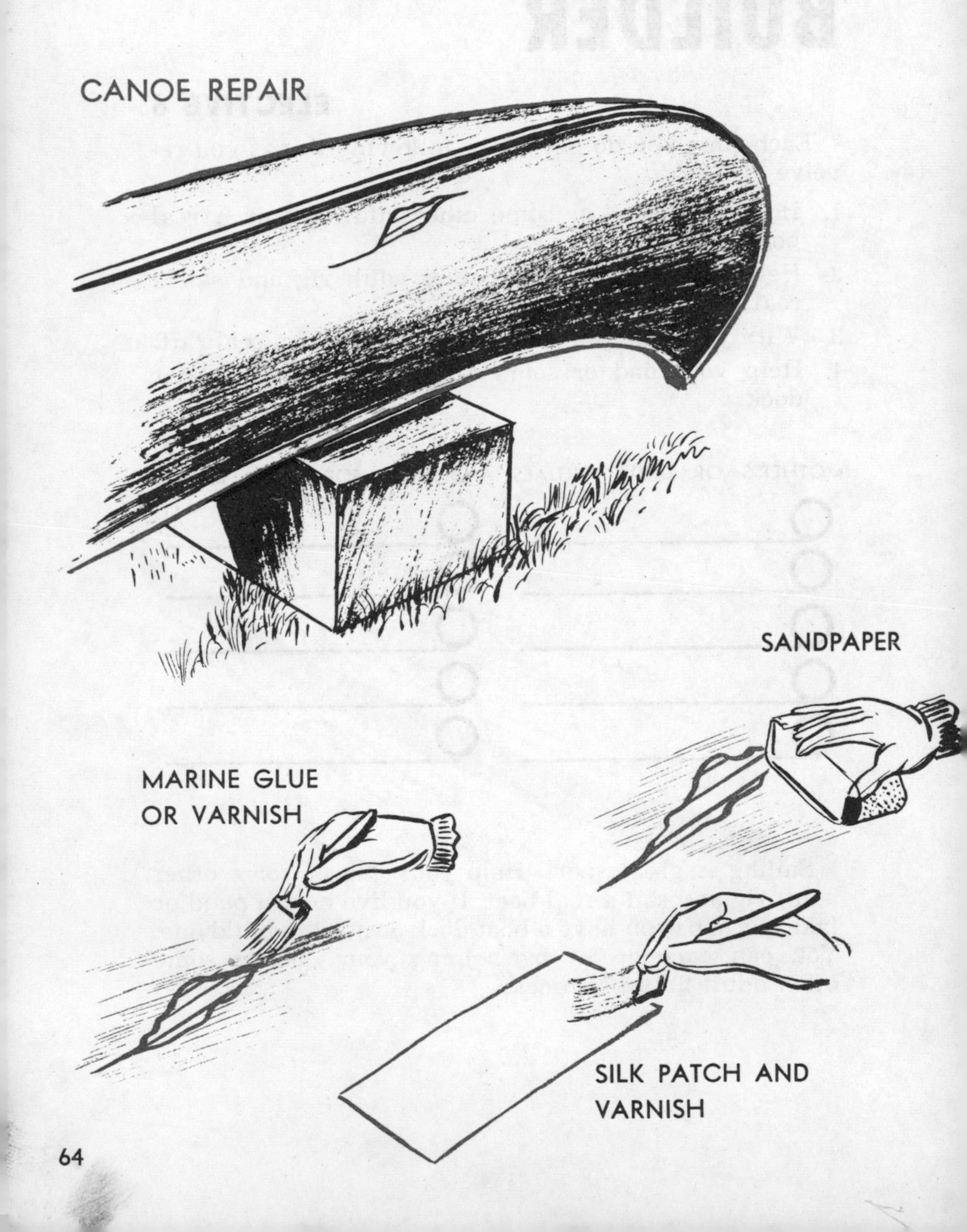

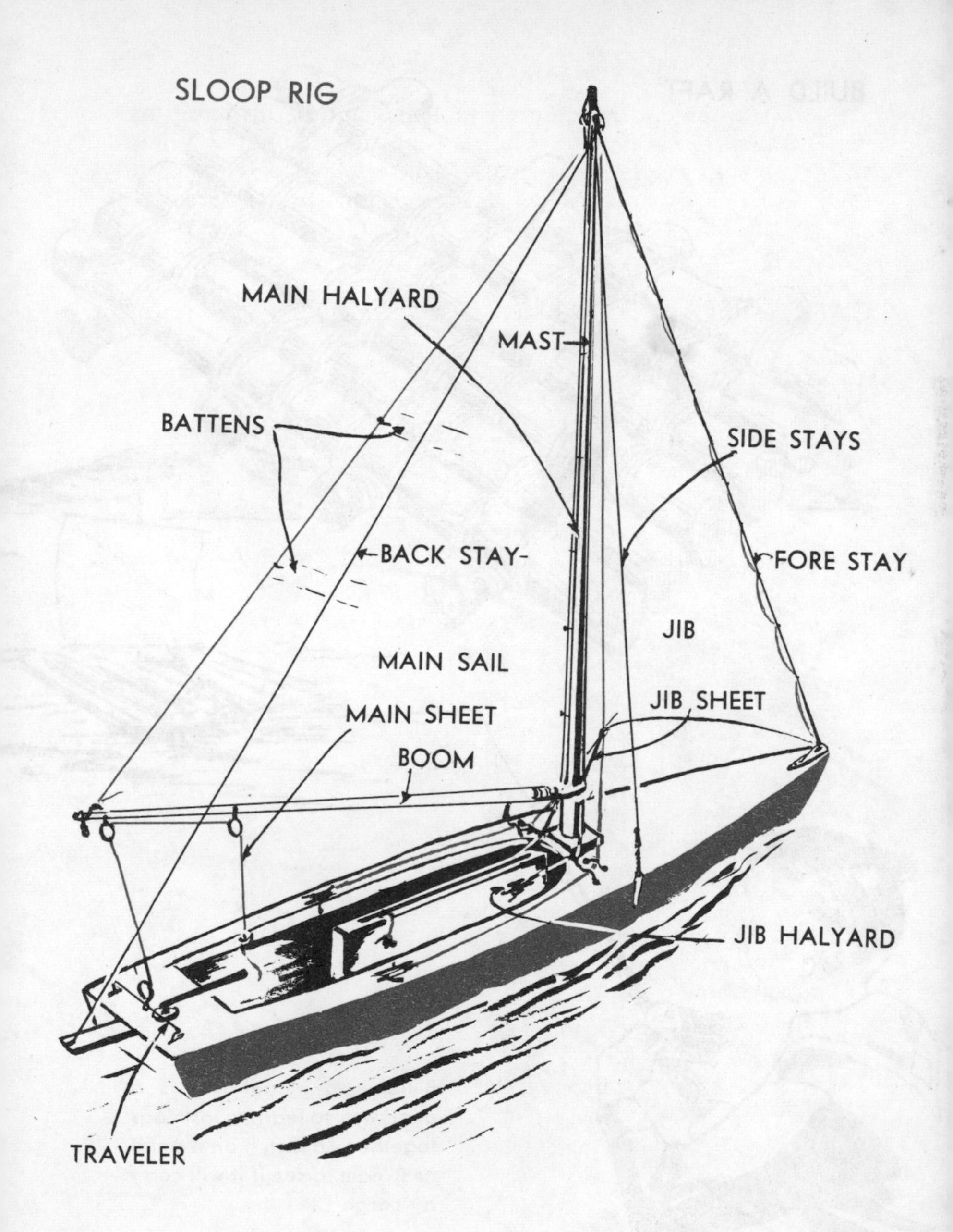
SLOOP RIG
MAIN HALYARD
MAST
BATTENS
SIDE STAYS
BACK STAY
FORE STAY
JIB
MAIN SAIL
JIB SHEET
MAIN SHEET
BOOM
JIB HALYARD
TRAVELER

BUILD A RAFT

Building a model raft is a good way to learn to lash logs together. Launch it on a pond or stream to see if it will carry a "cargo".

REPAIR A DOCK

SKY OBSERVER

ELECTIVE 7

Each time you do one of the following things you receive *one credit.*

1. Be able to identify five different kinds of aircraft. (Watch them in flight if you can, or from models or photos. This may be done for credit more than once if you identify different planes.)
2. Help make a pilot trainer.
3. Draw or make a map of the sky showing some planets and constellations.
4. Identify at night at least three planets that you can see without a telescope.
5. Demonstrate an eclipse of the sun.
6. Tell why you would like to go to any planet or moon that you choose.

MOTHER'S OR DAD'S INITIALS AND DATE FOR EACH CREDIT

(3) 2-2-58

TYPES OF PLANES

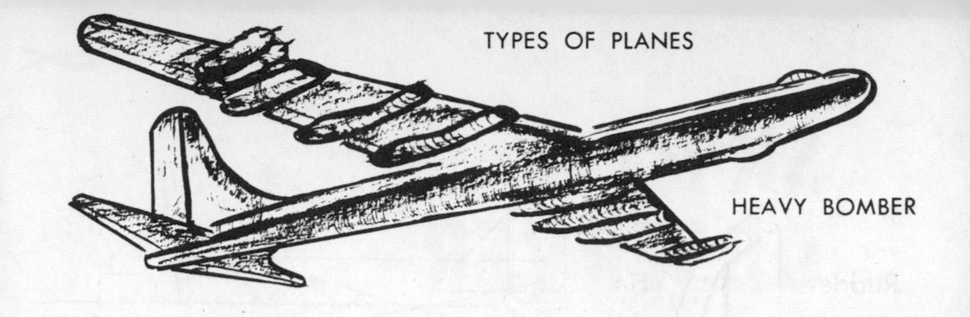

HEAVY BOMBER

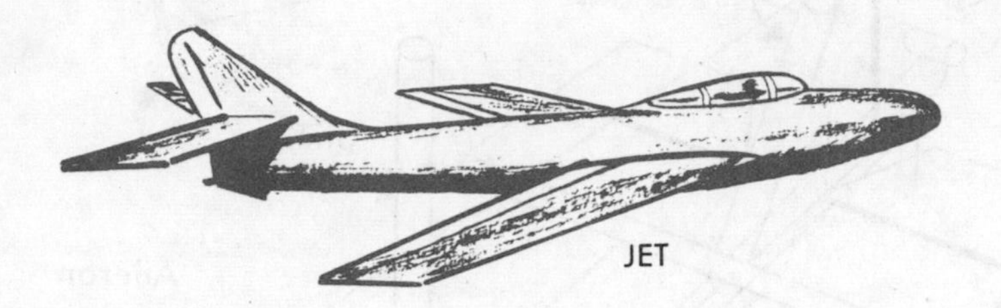

JET

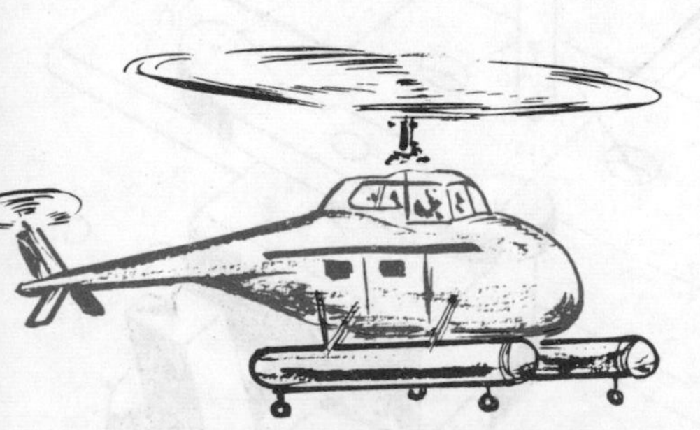

AMPHIBIOUS HELICOPTER

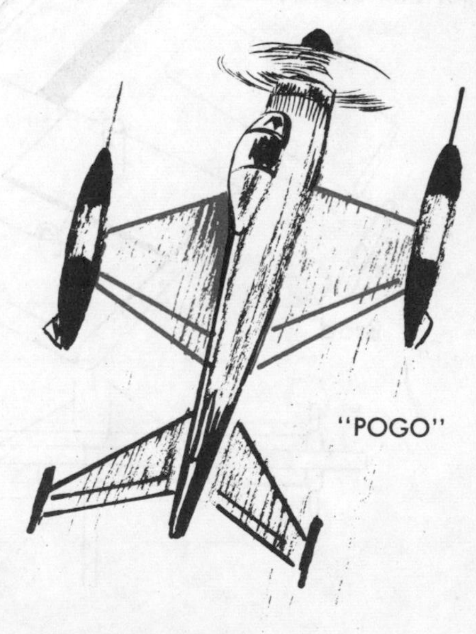

"POGO"

Did you ever think of fastening wires from corner to corner of the ceiling of your room and hanging up your scale model planes? You can paint them with bright colors and they'll really decorate your room.

FLYING BOAT

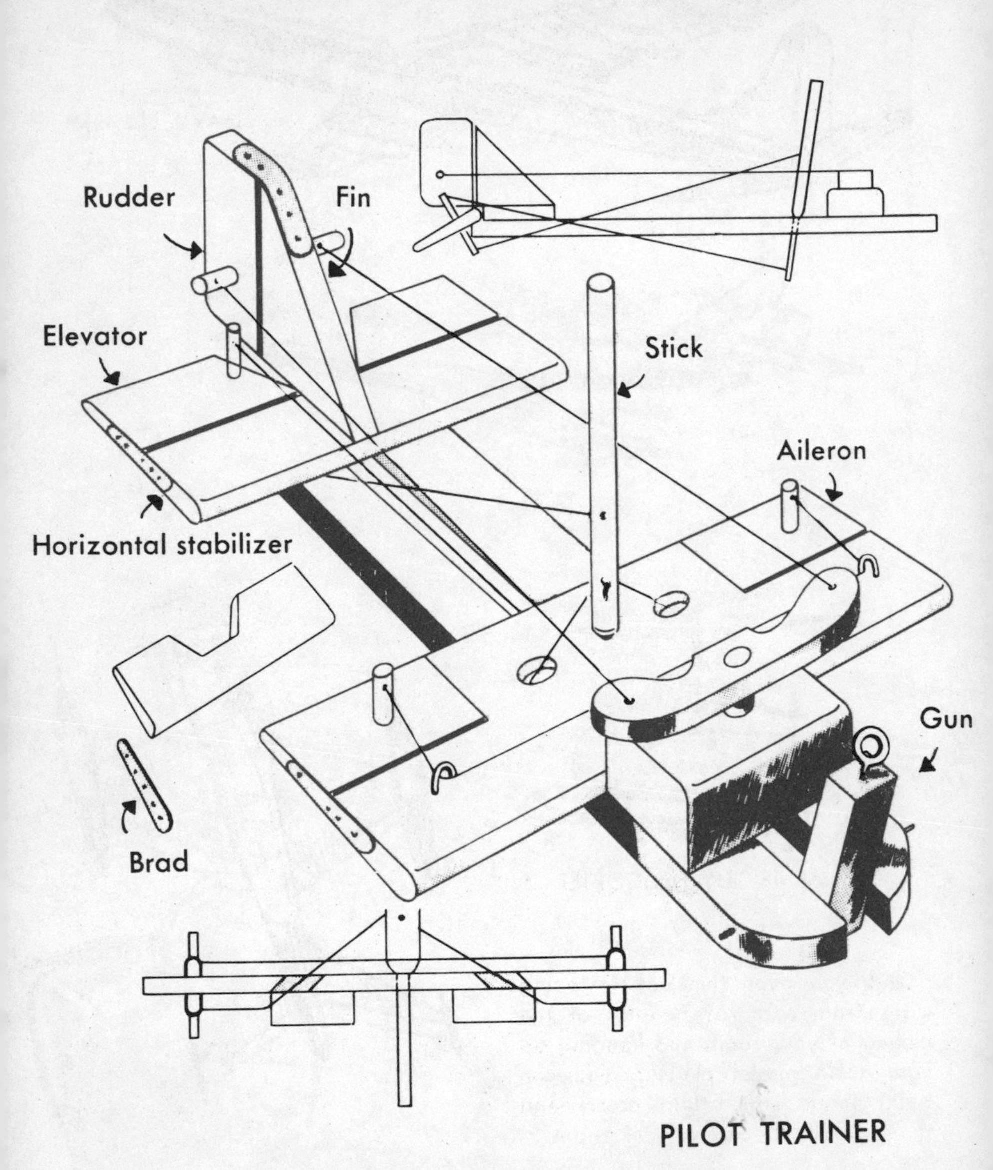

PILOT TRAINER

Sit at the controls of your own space ship and take off for the moon. Bank—climb—dive—and roll in this pilot trainer. Controls work just like a real ship.

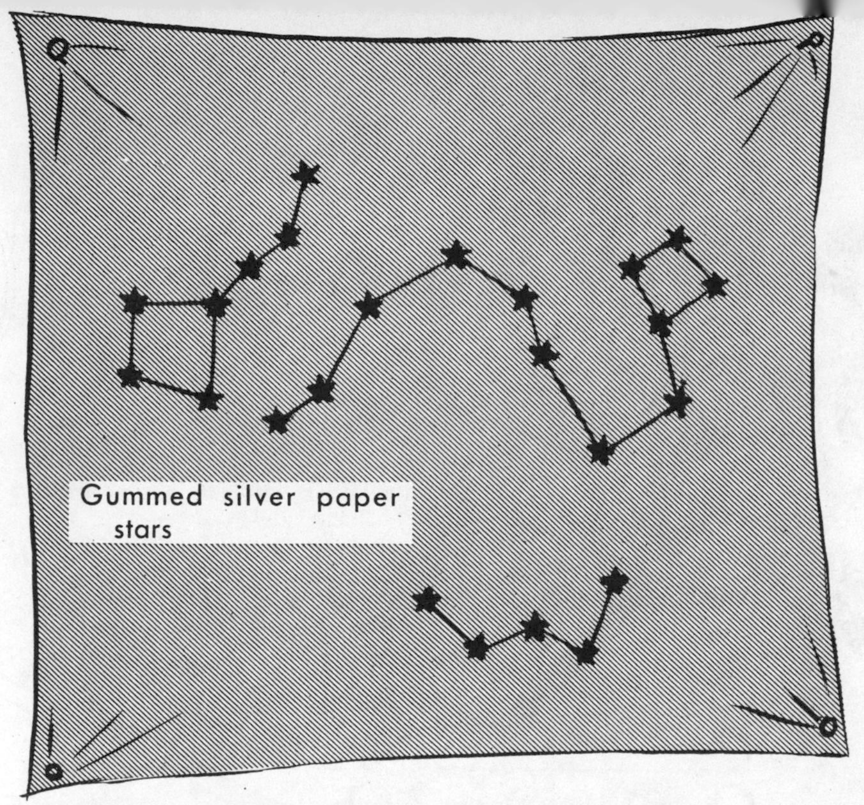

Navigators from the earliest times used the stars to guide them. Make up a sky map of all the planets you want to visit. Put them on your map in the right places.

Constellations punched as holes in tin cans

THINGS THAT GO

ELECTIVE 8

Each time you do one of the following things you receive *one credit.*

1. Make something you can ride on, such as a scooter, pushmobile or wagon.
2. Make a rocker-tilting game.

MOTHER'S OR DAD'S INITIALS AND DATE FOR EACH CREDIT

○ ____________________ ○ ____________________
○ ____________________ ○ ____________________
○ ____________________ ○ ____________________
○ ____________________ ○ ____________________
○ ____________________ ○ ____________________

ROCKER TILTING

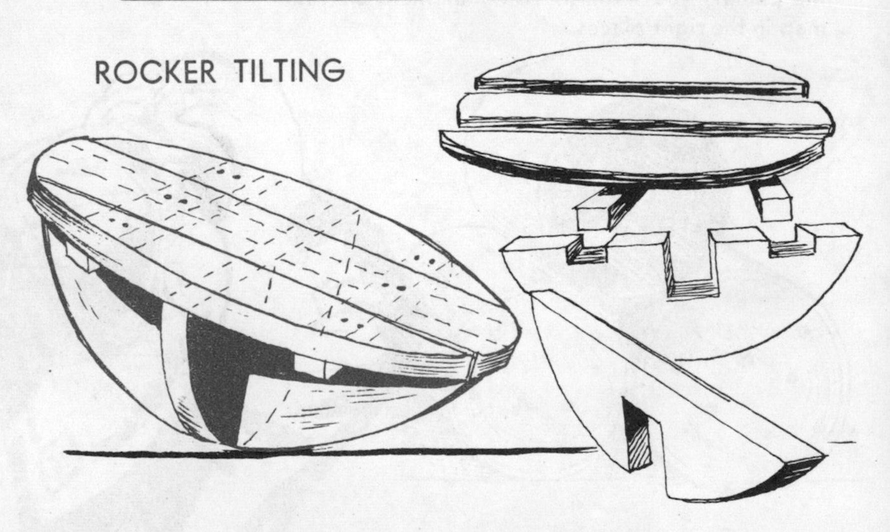

Have you ever heard of Soap Box Derbies? They are held all over America. Maybe you can't be the national winner. Maybe there isn't even a Soap Box Derby near you, but the boys of your Den can all make pushmobiles and have their own pushmobile races!

MECHANIC

ELECTIVE 9

Each time you do one of the following things you receive *one credit.*

1. Keep a bicycle in good condition and fix a tire. Tell what part of a bike has to be repaired by an expert repairman.
2. Help someone change a tire on a bicycle or an automobile. Explain how to do it.
3. Repair roller skates or scooter.

MOTHER'S OR DAD'S INITIALS AND DATE FOR EACH CREDIT

○ ________________ ○ ________________
○ ________________ ○ ________________
○ ________________ ○ ________________
○ ________________ ○ ________________
○ ________________ ○ ________________

A spoke wrench can be used to tighten spokes without taking the tire off the rim. With tire removed from rim, use screw driver.

TIRE REPAIR

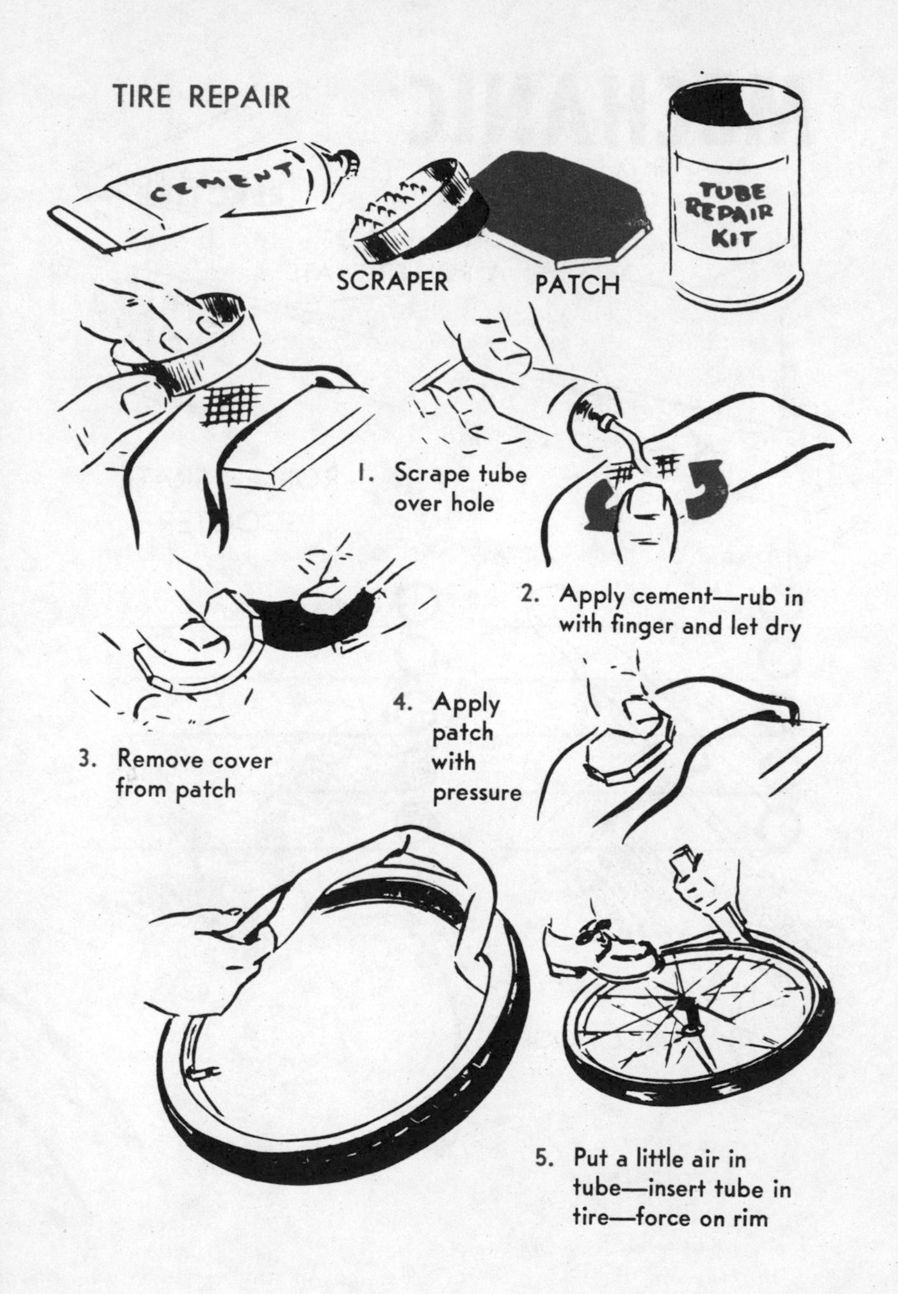
CEMENT
SCRAPER
PATCH
TUBE REPAIR KIT
1. Scrape tube over hole
2. Apply cement—rub in with finger and let dry
3. Remove cover from patch
4. Apply patch with pressure
5. Put a little air in tube—insert tube in tire—force on rim

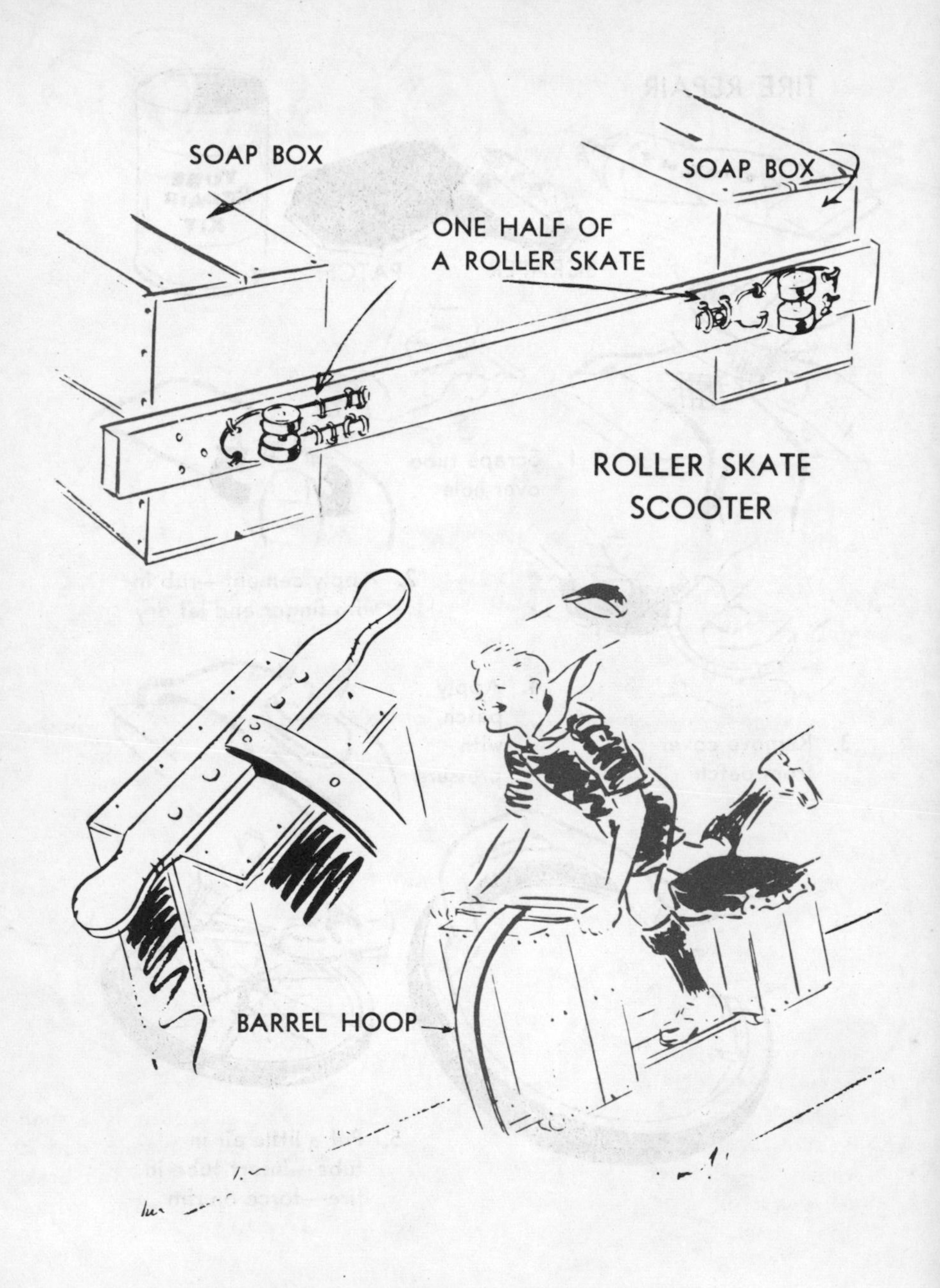
SOAP BOX
SOAP BOX
ONE HALF OF
A ROLLER SKATE
ROLLER SKATE
SCOOTER
BARREL HOOP

1. Insert jack. An axle jack is the safest kind.

2. Jack up the car until tire is off ground.

3. Remove hub cap.

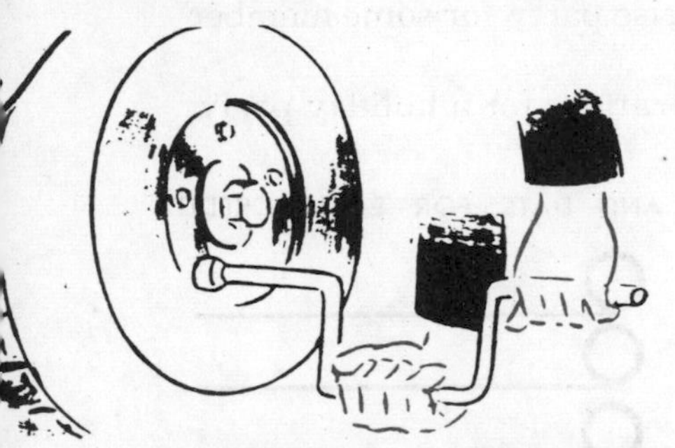

4. Loosen and remove bolts (or nuts). Put them in hub cap.

5. You can use a block of wood and short plank to help lift weight of wheel so it can be taken off.

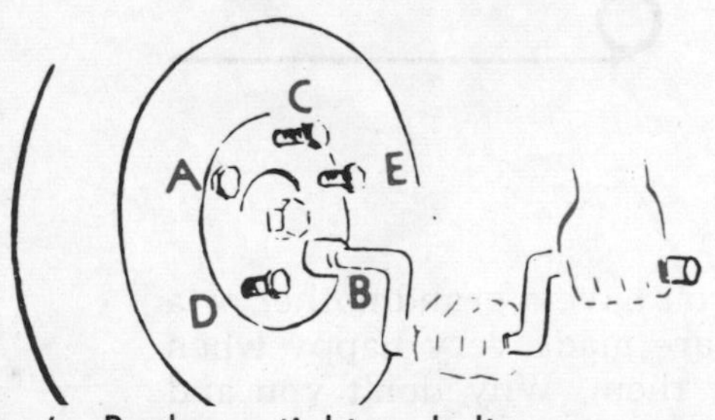

6. Replace, tighten bolts or nuts opposite one another.
7. Be sure brake is still on and wheels are blocked so the car won't roll when the jack is let down.

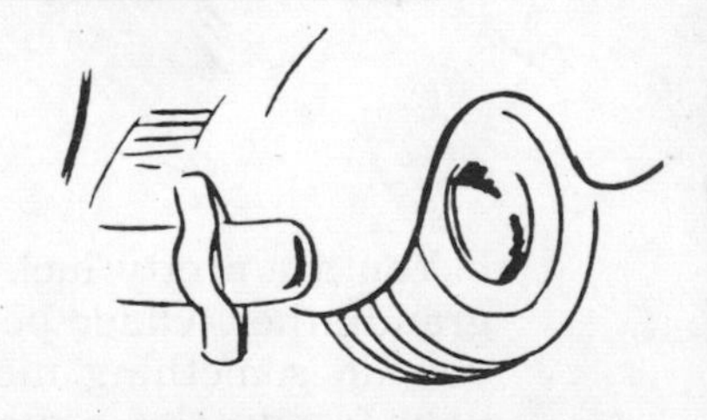

Changing an auto tire is a man-sized job, but you can help dad or mother. First, be sure the hand brake is on and wheels are blocked to prevent rolling off the jack.

PARTY GIVER

ELECTIVE 10

Each time you do one of the following things you receive *one credit.*

1. Help plan and run a surprise party for some member of your family.
2. Plan and make table decorations for a holiday party.

MOTHER'S OR DAD'S INITIALS AND DATE FOR EACH CREDIT

(2) 11-29-57 VRC
(2) 1-31-58 VRC
(1) 7-31-58 VRC

You are pretty lucky if you have a grandmother or a grandfather. Older people are made very happy when you do something nice for them. Why don't you and your family plan a special party for your grandmother? You don't have to wait for her birthday—just surprise her sometime. And make some of the things for the party. You can fix up the table with all sorts of decorations. Mother will help you.

If you don't have a grandmother or a grandfather, do the same thing for someone else in your family or some older person who doesn't have a grandson to give a party for him.

Learn how to set the table for a party, forks to the left of plate, knife and spoons to the right. Centerpiece goes in the middle, place cards by each plate.

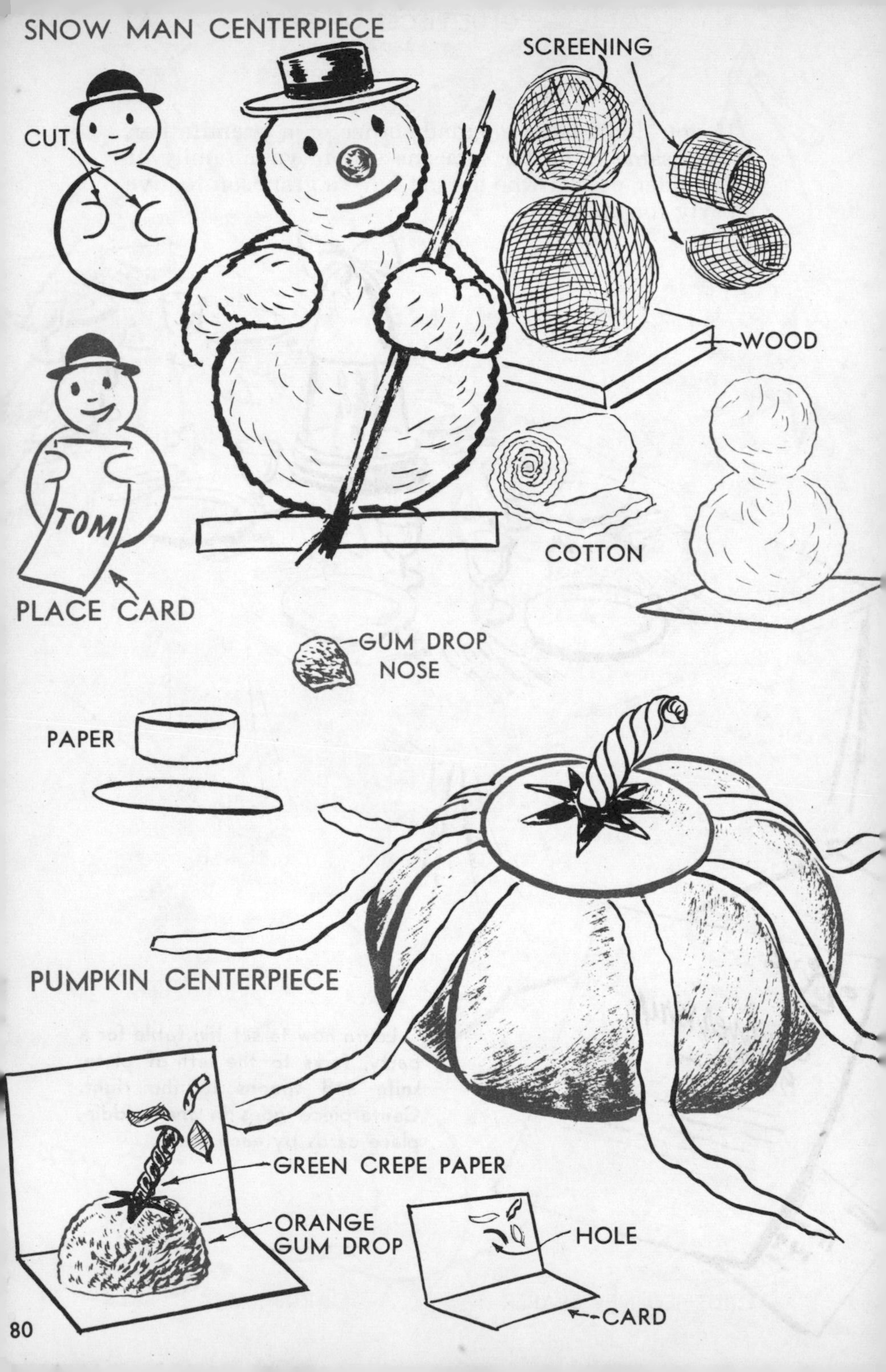
SNOW MAN CENTERPIECE
CUT
PLACE CARD
TOM
SCREENING
WOOD
COTTON
GUM DROP NOSE
PAPER
PUMPKIN CENTERPIECE
GREEN CREPE PAPER
ORANGE GUM DROP
HOLE
CARD

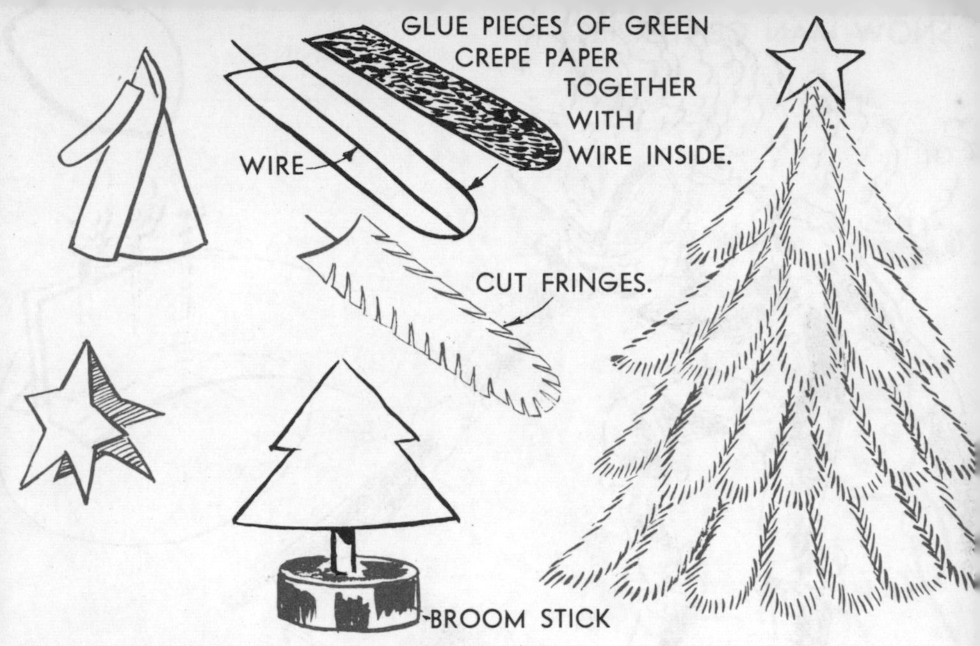

CHRISTMAS TREE CENTERPIECE

Invitations do much to make the spirit of the party. Ask mother to help you with some ideas.

Centerpieces add color to any table. Fruit, colored candles, even jars of colored water can be used effectively.

Gay, colorful, fun-loving favors brighten up each place and bring joy to the hearts of those who receive them. They're worth the time it takes to make them.

Place cards carry out the holiday mood and make each person feel welcome.

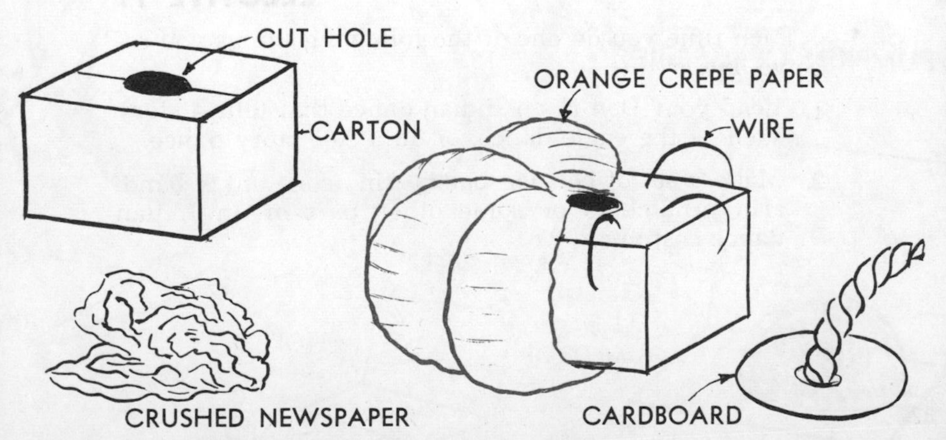

INDIAN DANCER

ELECTIVE 11

Each time you do one of the following things you receive *one credit*.

1. Lead your Den in an Indian dance that tells a story such as the eagle dance, or do a solo story dance.
2. Make a set of bell leg bands, tin cone ankle band, arm ornaments or some other part of an Indian dance costume.

MOTHER'S OR DAD'S INITIALS AND DATE FOR EACH CREDIT

○	○
○	○
○	○
○	○
○	○

Indian dance accessories are easy to make. Keep in mind that they take a lot of jarring and bouncing during your dance, so make them well. Take your time and tie all knots securely. Fasten feathers and beads on carefully.

You probably want to look back into your Wolf and Bear books for other Indian ideas, such as shields, tomahawks, tom-toms, Indian rattles and war clubs. You can find additional Indian dances in the *Golden Book of Indian Craft and Lore*, by Ben Hunt.

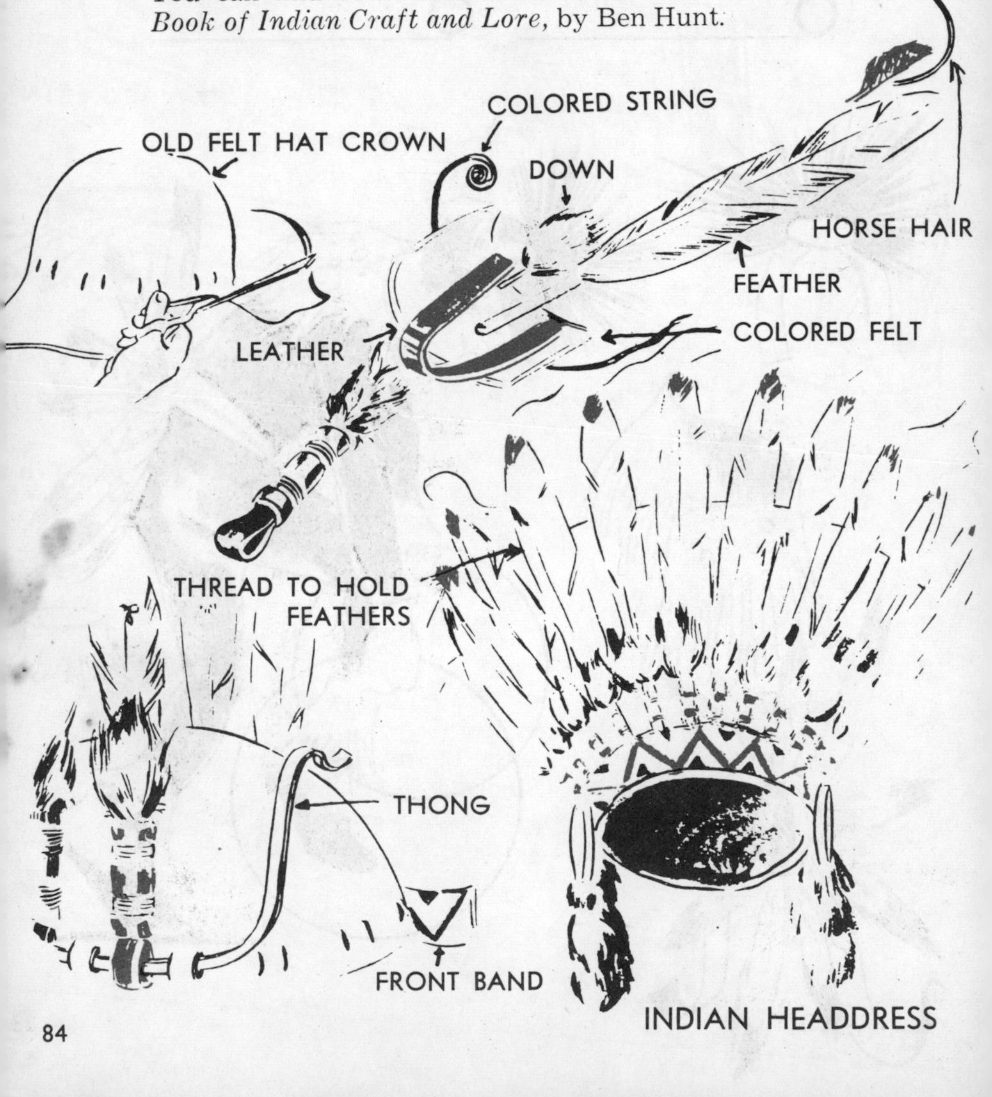

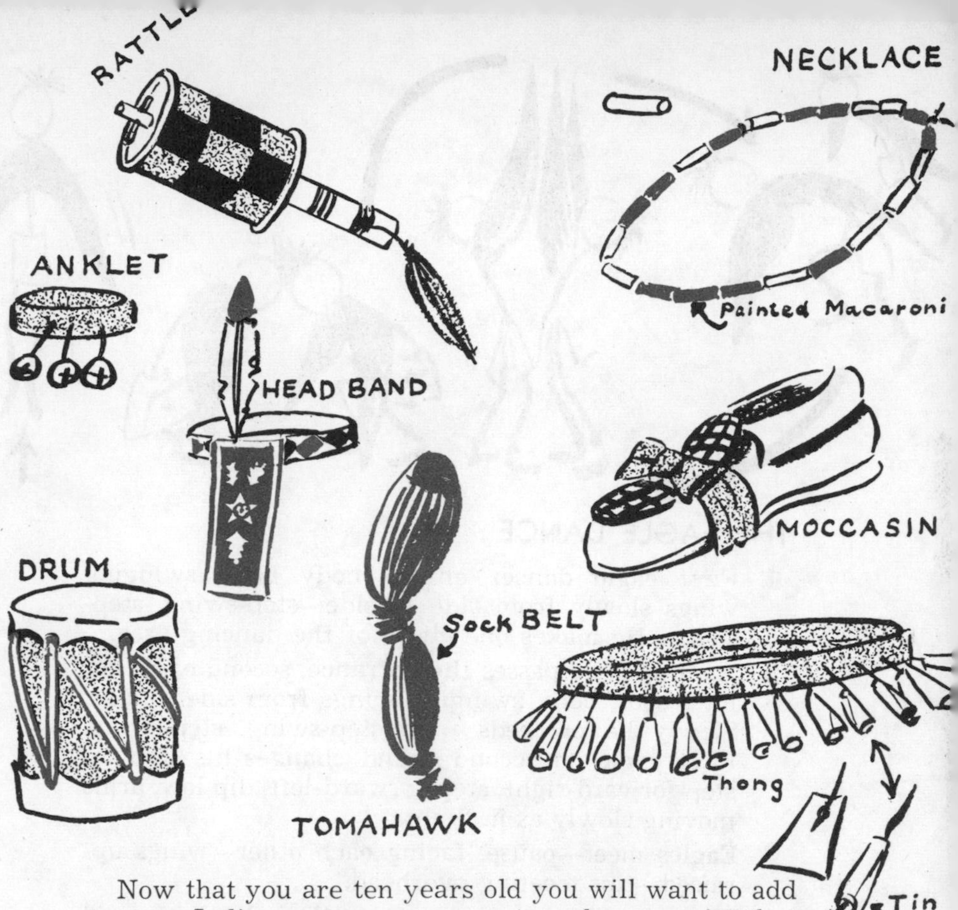

Now that you are ten years old you will want to add to your Indian costume ornaments and accessories that will make it something you can wear with pride. You will be able to use it in Indian ceremonies when you become a Boy Scout, too, for they have the "Great Spirit" at their campfires.

You will also be able to do better Indian dance steps now that you are older. Read over the legends on the next few pages. Learn the steps and lead your Den in the dance at some Pack meeting.

The Indian dance has long been a means of expressing hope and fear, inviting the blessing of the "Great Spirit," telling a story, preparing for the hunt, exciting a war party, or showing pure joy and thanksgiving.

THE EAGLE DANCE

1. First eagle dancer enters, body bent, swinging wings slowly from side to side—step-swing, step-swing. He makes one circle of the dancing area.
2. As first eagle passes the entrance, second eagle enters, body bent, swinging wings from side to side. Slowly he proceeds with step-swing, step-swing. First eagle on second round changes his step to: step-forward-right, step-forward-left, dip low, arms moving slowly as in flight.
3. Eagles meet—pause, facing each other—wings upraised—tips meeting overhead.
4. They cautiously circle each other, lowering and raising the wings.
5. They each complete their circle.
6. Facing each other again they pause, beating their wings and squatting.
7. Feet close together, each eagle hops to his own right, flopping wings challengingly.
8. Hop, Hop, Hop, to his own left.
9. Hop, Hop, Hop, to his own right.
10. Hop, Hop, Hop, to his own left.
11. Calmly now they inspect each other as they again circle around.

12. The first eagle starts to circle the area. The second eagle pauses briefly, then turns and follows the first eagle. On second round they step together, one behind the other, wings slightly overlapping.
13. With high hop-point step, progress to the right—hop on left foot, at the same time raise right knee high in front, tap with right toe, feet close together. To left—forward—back. Eagles make all movements at the same time.
14. Facing each other, softly sway the wings parallel to each other.
15. Turn and exit using the step-and-dip (2), wings overlapping.

Solo dancing gives you an opportunity to dance out a story. You are limited only by your imagination and the dancing area.

Make up a story of a hunt, an Indian legend or an appeal to the "Great Spirit," add signs such as looking, testing the soil, resting, shooting or whatever others will tell YOUR story, then adapt your steps to fit your action. Several steps are shown on this page. Read *Rhythm of the Redman,* by Julia M. Buttree, and *Handicraft* by Lester Griswold.

THE INITIATION OF LITTLE BEAR

The day has come for the young Chippewa brave, Little Bear, to be initiated into the Midewiwin—the Grand Medicine Society. He has been taught by the leader that long life comes of leading a good life, that those who lie and steal will be punished. There is much singing and dancing and feasting.

Little Bear sits on a pile of blankets at the foot of the medicine pole. Otter Tail, one of the initiators, blows on his medicine bag and walks toward Little Bear, shouting, "We-ho-ho-ho-ho!" Suddenly he "shoots" Little Bear, thrusting the medicine bag toward him with a yell. Little Bear "feels" the shot and falls flat on the ground. All of the initiators then gather around, place their medicine bags on the back of Little Bear, and sing this song in a high, throbbing tone:

(Wi-na-ke means *"I have shot straight"*)

At the end of the song, Little Bear is raised to his feet. He has been "shot" with medicine, and is now ready to become one of the Midewiwin.

THE FEATHER THAT CHANGED A MAN

(A Chippewa Indian Legend)

Once there were two Indians who were close friends. The older man was very grouchy toward everyone, and he would not believe anything that anybody told him. Therefore, he was not very well liked. The younger man, however, was just the opposite, and he got along well with everybody.

One day the young Indian took a thread from the clothing of his friend and went to a wise old Medicine Man, asking him to use his great power to change the ways of his friend and make him more agreeable.

The Medicine Man took a feather, cut a slit in the quill and put the thread inside the quill along with a little medicine. Then he fastened the quill together so the cut could not be seen. After singing a song of good medicine, he gave the young Indian this feather, and also another feather which looked just like the first one, but which had no medicine in it.

On his return, the young man gave his friend the feather with medicine in it. And each of the Indians wore one of the feathers in his hair. After a time the older man began to be more cheerful and kind toward everyone, until finally he was entirely changed. This was the work of the medicine and the Medicine Man's song.

MUSICIAN

ELECTIVE 12

Each time you do one of the following things you receive *one credit*:

1. Play a regular musical instrument.
   (You may do this more than once if you use different kinds of instruments.)
2. Make up a Cub Scout song and teach it to your Den.
3. With your Den, put on a Cub Scout opera or variety show.

MOTHER'S OR DAD'S INITIALS AND DATE FOR EACH CREDIT

1 11-6-57 VRC

WE'RE GLAD TO SEE YOU HERE

Tune: Farmer in the Dell

We're glad to see you here,
It gives us joy and cheer,
Sure, it's true, we say to you,
We're glad to see you here.

Make up a Cub Scout song that tells about your Den or Pack, about something they did, about your fellow Cub Scouts in the Den, or compose a song about the Cub Scout Promise or the Law of the Pack.

Get your mother or Den Mother to help you work up a Cub Scout opera or variety show. Maybe your music teacher can help you with some ideas.

MASKS

ELECTIVE 13

Each time you do one of the following things you receive *one credit:*

1. Make a simple papier maché head.
2. Make a mask.
3. Make a "Hopi" Indian mask.
4. Draw, paint, or crayon three designs of native ceremonial masks.

MOTHER'S OR DAD'S INITIALS AND DATE FOR EACH CREDIT

(2) 2-2-58 VRC
(4) 5-2-58 VRC

Follow the simple steps shown here for making a built-up mask. You can make any kind of character head this way. Be patient, put on several layers for strength, let dry several days before painting.

HOPI INDIAN MASKS are used in ceremonial dances. Go to your library and look them up in the Indian books.

Ask your librarian for a book on ceremonial masks. You'll find several native designs that will be fun to make or to copy.

You can make solid papier maché heads by letting your newspaper pieces soak in thin paste for two or three days and modelling the heads out of the pulpy mass just as you would in working with clay.

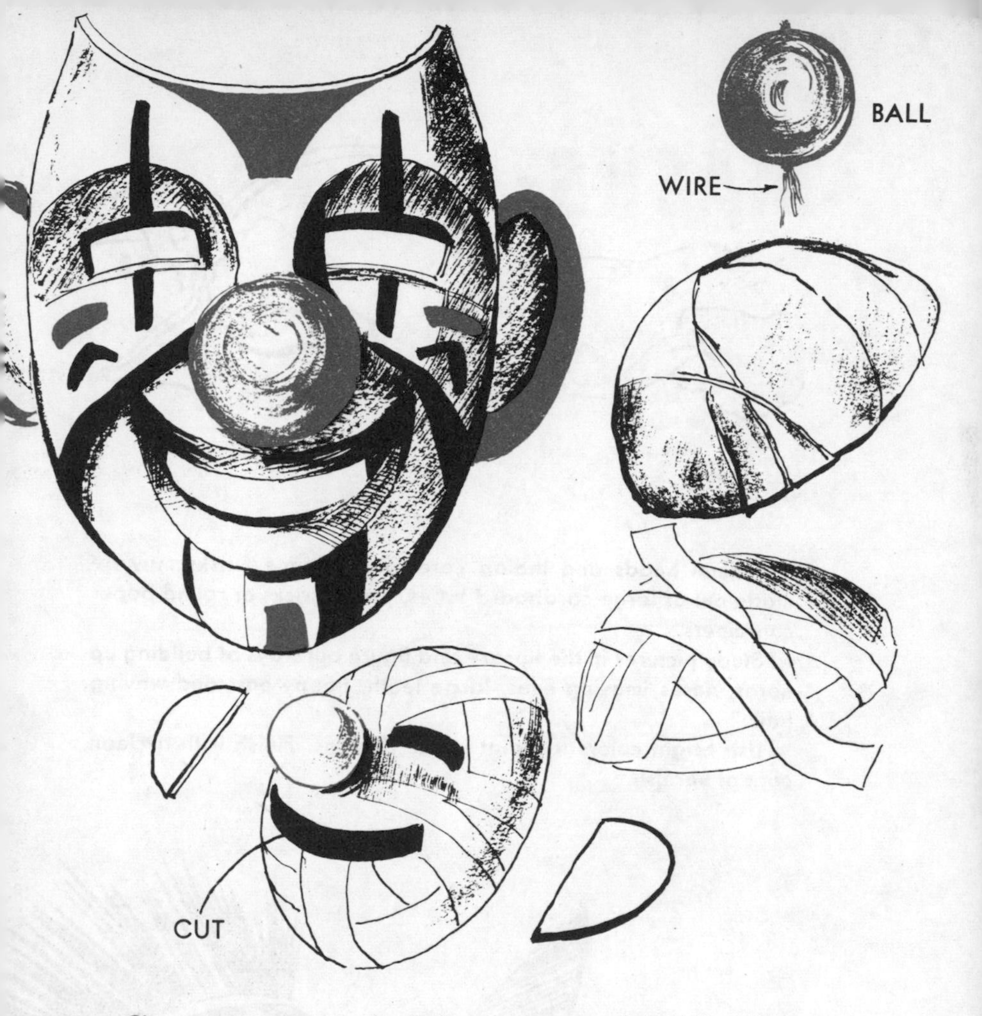

Character masks may be built up on an oval dish. Turn dish upside down—grease it—then start to build up layers of papier-mache. To build up eyebrows, noses, thick lips or round cheeks, hold wads of newspaper or bunches of excelsior in place, then paste down with long strips of paper. Add several alternate layers for greater strength. After it is completely dry, paint in additional features.

You can use rubber ball for clown nose, rope yarn or broom straws for hair.

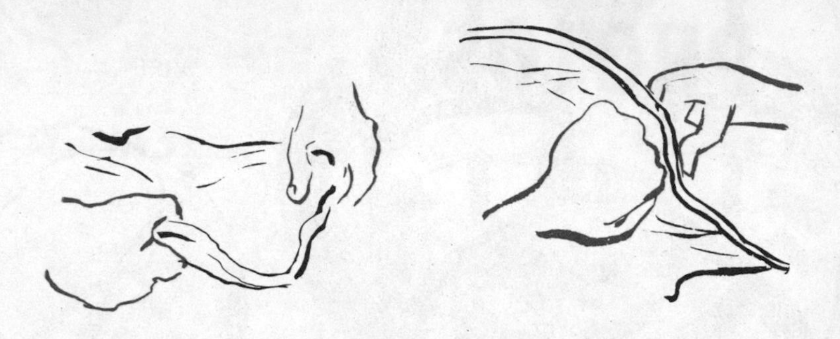

Animal heads and Indian ceremonial dance masks may be made out of large cardboard tubes, paper sacks or round paper containers.

Study pictures in the library and figure out ways of building up horns, noses, moving eyes, large teeth, floppy ears and waving hair.

Use bright colors to paint in the designs. Finish with a clean coat of varnish.

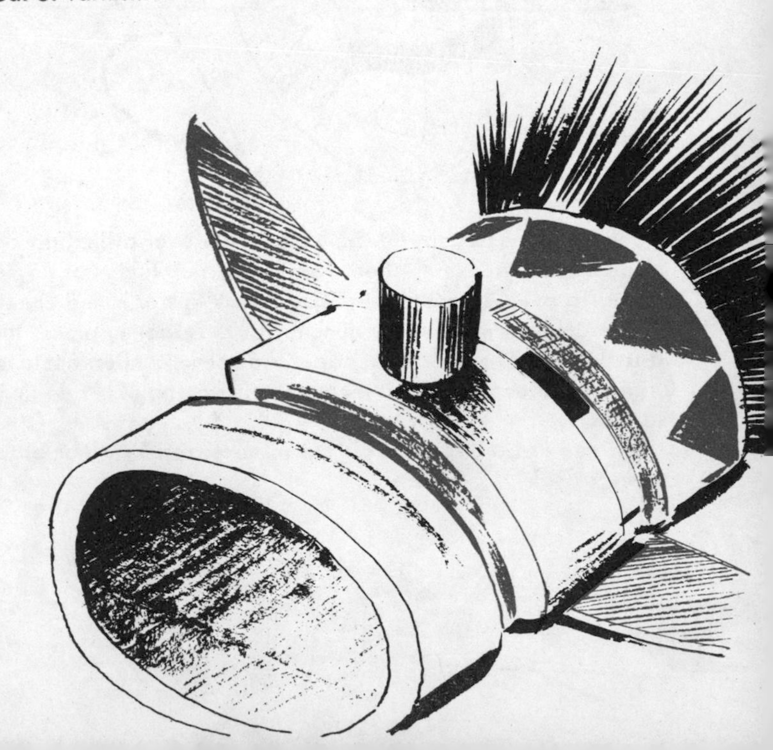

PHOTOS

ELECTIVE 14

Each time you do one of the following things you receive *one credit:*

1. Take a roll of films and process the negatives.
2. Show how you can improve pictures printed from these negatives by careful cropping.

MOTHER'S OR DAD'S INITIALS AND DATE FOR EACH CREDIT

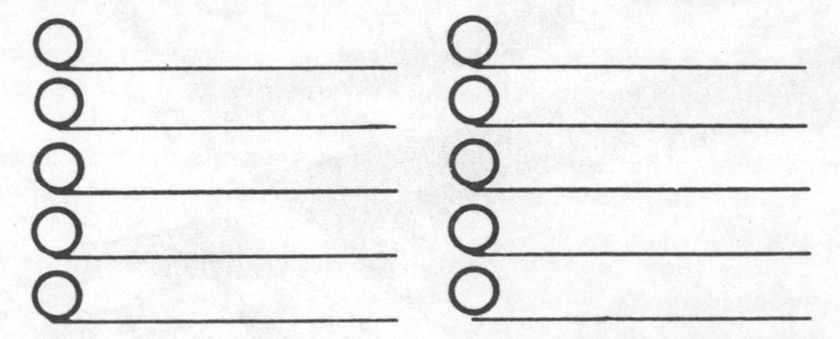

Why don't you try to take some pictures of animals or birds? It's fun. Have dad help you make a blind near your bird feeding station.

With the help of your dad or mother fix up a place for a dark room and a box in which to store the things you will need to do your own developing and printing.

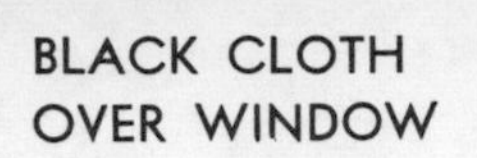

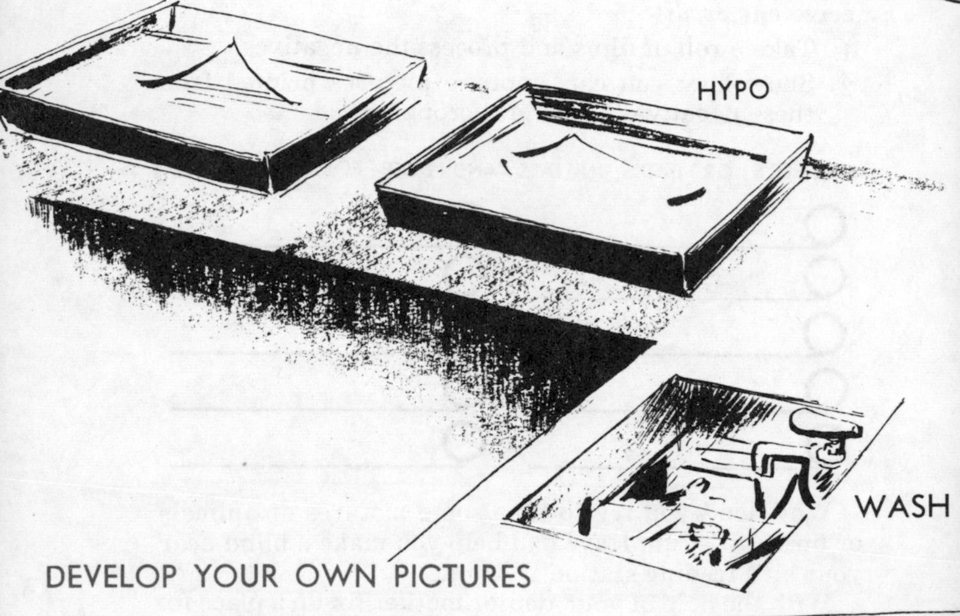

DEVELOP YOUR OWN PICTURES

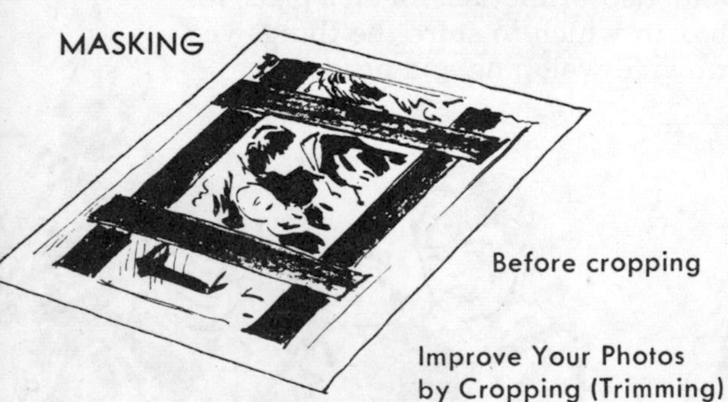

Before cropping

Improve Your Photos
by Cropping (Trimming)

After cropping

NATURE

ELECTIVE 15

Each time you do one of the following you receive *one credit:*

1. Find an insect cocoon and keep it to see what happens.
2. Find a caterpillar and keep it for a week.
3. Catch some snails, a salamander or a lizard and keep for a month.
4. Keep a turtle as a pet for a month.
5. Make an ant house and keep some ants in it.
6. Keep some crickets or a praying mantis for a month.
7. Make a butterfly collection.
8. Keep some tadpoles and watch them develop.

MOTHER'S OR DAD'S INITIALS AND DATE FOR EACH CREDIT

4 11-6-57 V.R.C.

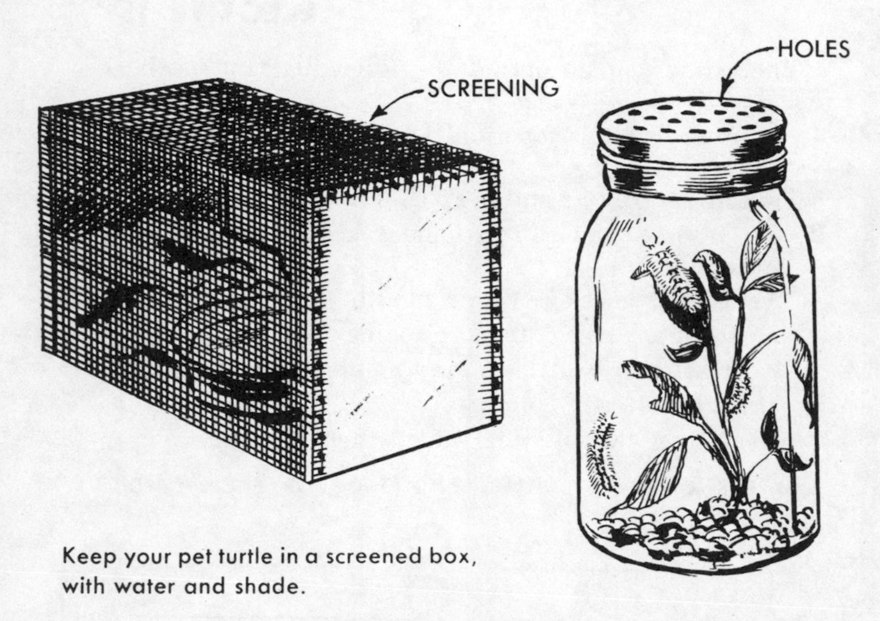

Keep your pet turtle in a screened box, with water and shade.

CATERPILLAR HOUSE

FILL JAR WITH LEAVES, PUNCH HOLES IN JAR LID FOR AIR.

Another nature idea that's good fun is a nature hunt. Maybe you can have a dad and son nature hunt with your Den. In a nature hunt, a trail is laid out ahead of time, and signs are put up telling what to do and what to find. Then you Cub Scouts and your dads follow the trail, one at a time, and stop at each sign, doing what it tells you.

Look under old logs, rocks, or in holes in the ground for ant nest. Scoop up as many of the ants as you can and place them in your ant house. Feed ants mash made from corn meal, pieces of cookie, a few drops of molasses or honey, small bits of meat or bread crumbs.

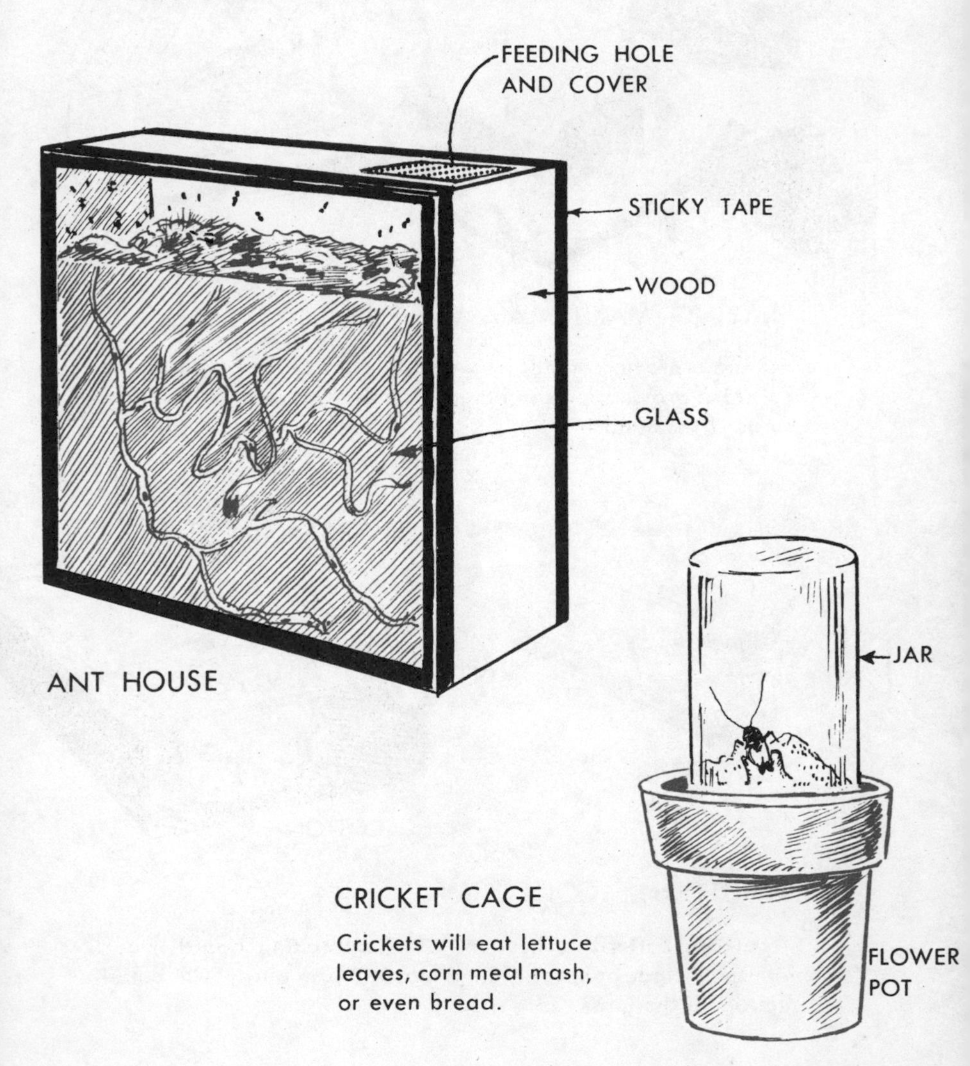

CRICKET CAGE

Crickets will eat lettuce leaves, corn meal mash, or even bread.

PRAYING MANTIS AS A PET

Keep a praying mantis between the window and the screen.

Feed it grasshoppers or other soft insects, or small bits of hamburger from hand.

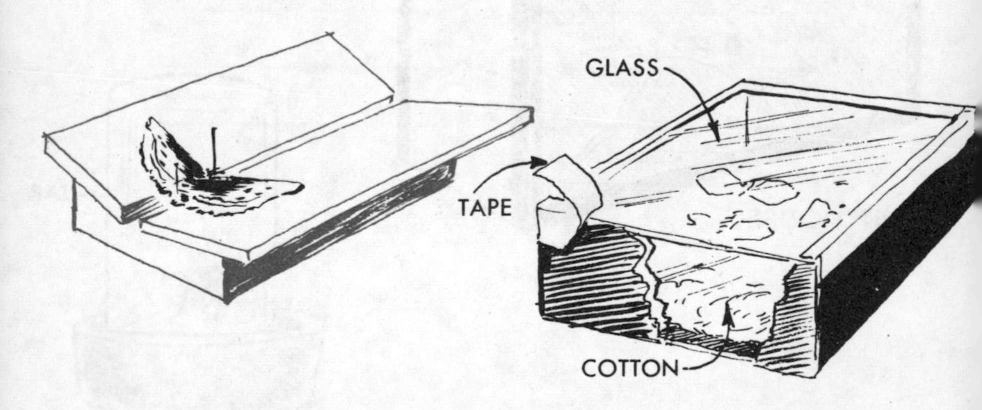

A BUTTERFLY COLLECTION

Make a butterfly collection. Get a spreading board; mount with small cigar box, cotton and glass. Or use a tray with butterflies under the glass.

DOGS

ELECTIVE 16

Each time you do one of the following things you receive *one credit:*

1. Take care of a dog for a month.
2. Read a book about a dog.
3. Name six different kinds of dogs and tell what they are used for. (Sheep dogs, pointers, retrievers, hounds, etc.)
4. Teach a dog to do a simple trick.
5. Know what to do about a "mad" dog.

MOTHER'S OR DAD'S INITIALS AND DATE FOR EACH CREDIT

3 11-2-57 V.R.C.

2 10-15-57 V.R.C.

5 11-2-57 V.R.C.

Even if you don't have a dog of your own, perhaps you can take care of one that belongs to a neighbor or relative. Taking care of a dog means feeding it the right kinds of food regularly, giving it water every day, seeing that it gets plenty of exercise, and giving it a bath in the proper way every so often. It may also mean taking the dog to a doctor if it gets sick, or taking proper steps to see that it does not get sick. If there is an animal doctor in your neighborhood, talk with him about how to take care of a dog. These pictures show a few different kinds of dogs. Look around your neighborhood and you'll see others.

FOX TERRIER

AIRDALE

DALMATIAN

BEAGLE

ENGLISH SETTER

Courtesy of LIFE Magazine
Drawings by Edwin Megargee

Your school library will probably have some books about dogs. Ask your teacher or mother to help you find one.

Simple tricks to teach dogs are: teaching it to bring back a ball you throw, teaching it to "beg" for food, teaching it to play dead or lie down at your command, or teaching it to walk at your heels when you go for a walk.

The best thing to do about a "mad" dog is to get away as fast as possible. But WALK away, quietly and carefully so you don't attract his attention. Go in the house and close the door. Call a policeman.

LANDSCAPER

ELECTIVE 17

Each time you do one of the following things you receive *one credit:*

1. Help your parents take care of your lawn for the season: Seed bare spots, fight quack grass, fight dandelions. Agree ahead of time on what you will do.
2. 4-H project (if you are a member).
3. Help spray against insects.

MOTHER'S OR DAD'S INITIALS AND DATE FOR EACH CREDIT

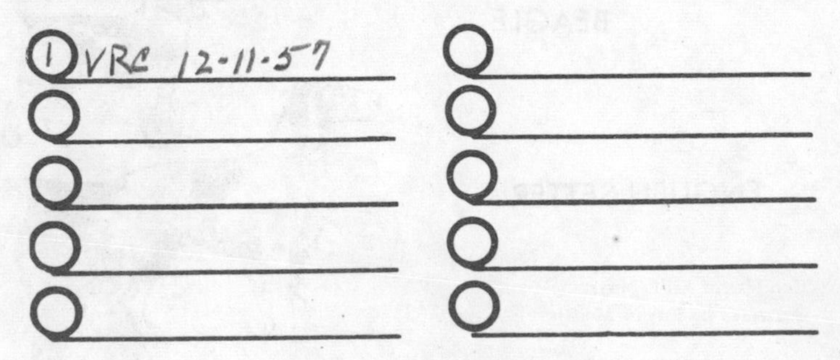

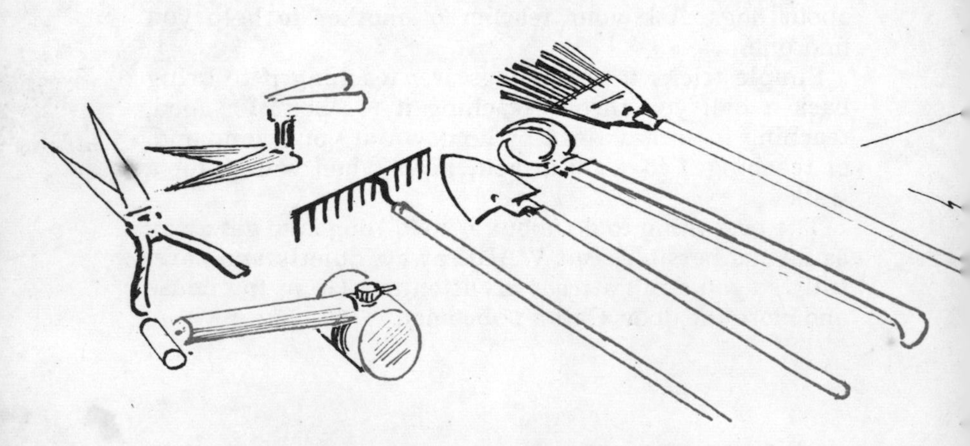

SOIL AND WATER CONSERVATION

ELECTIVE 18

Each time you do one of the following things you receive *one credit:*

1. Dig a hole deep enough to find at least two layers of soil. Describe the difference you see and feel in the layers.

2. Place some soil from each layer in a pot or box and plant a bean seed in each soil sample. After a month, tell which kind of soil grew the best-looking plant.

3. Make a simple rain gauge and find out how much rain falls in a week.

4. Draw a simple picture that shows how water that falls as rain gets to your water tap.

5. Carry out an experiment that shows how soil may be lost or ruined.

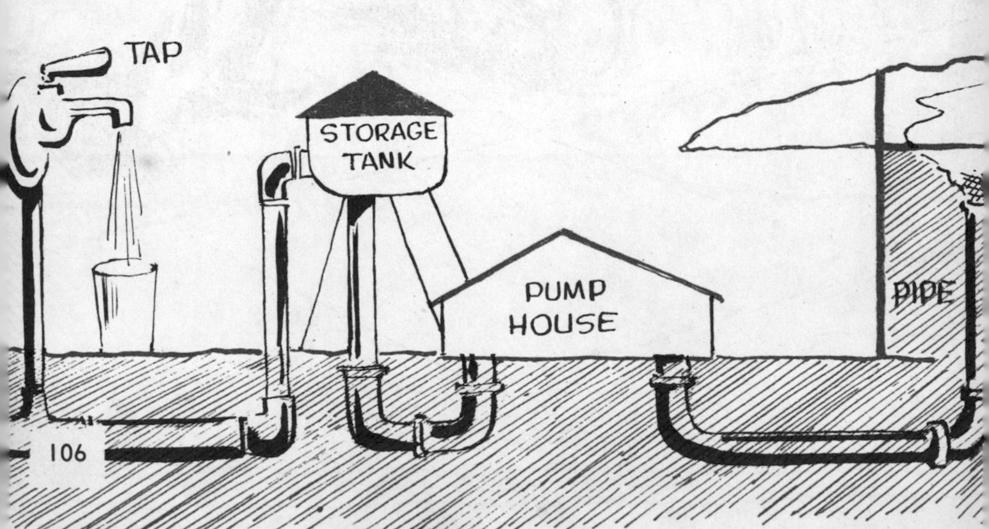

MOTHER'S OR DAD'S INITIALS AND DATE FOR EACH CREDIT

(4) 2-15-58 VRC.

(1) 5-10-58 VRC

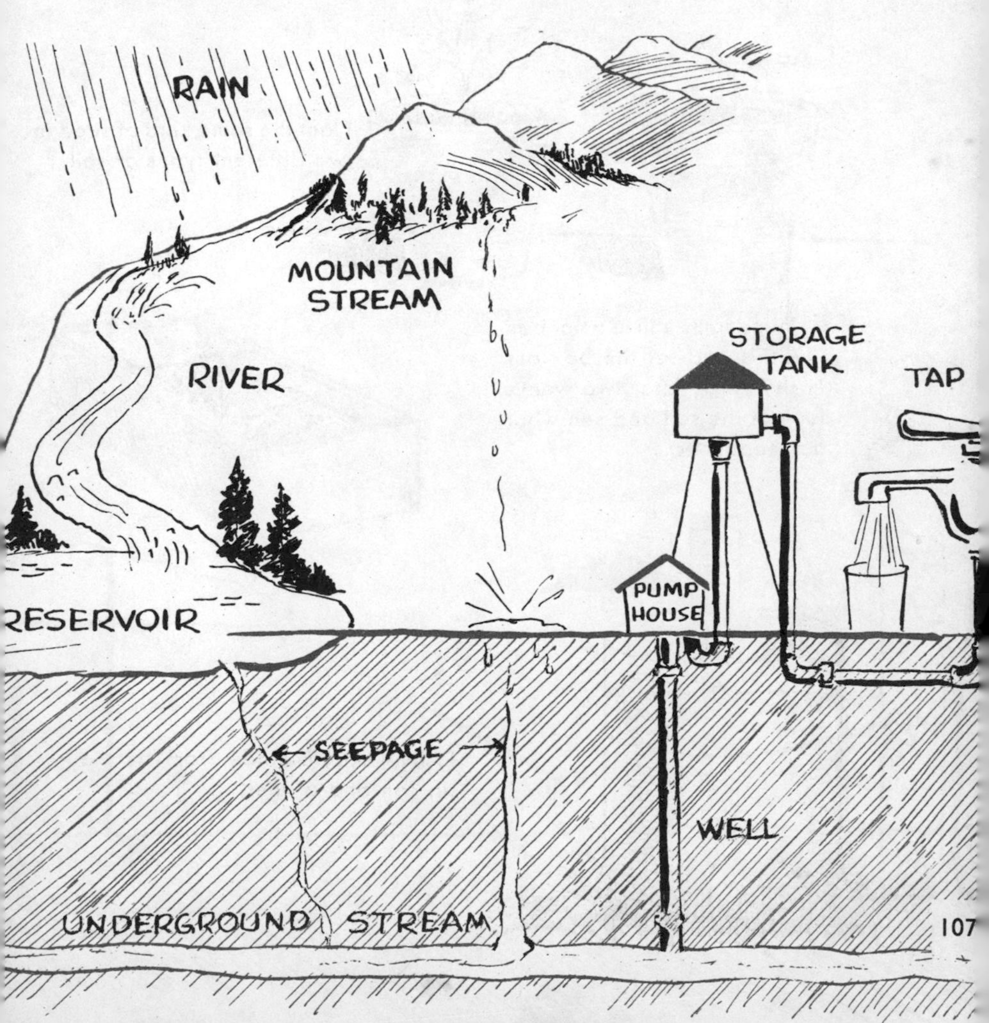

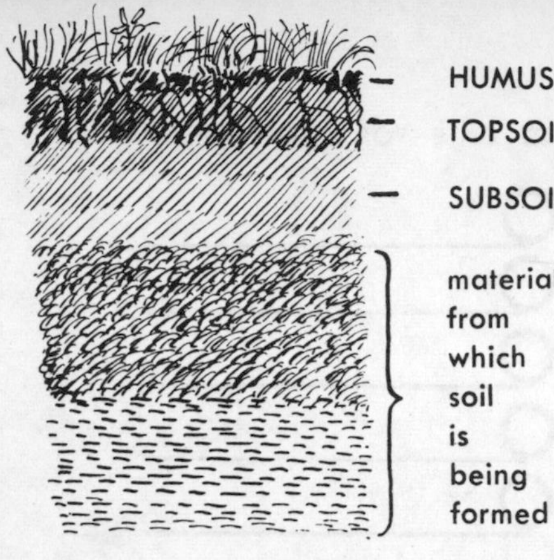

Soil is very important to you. All your food and almost all your clothing come from plants that grow in soil and from animals that eat plants that grow in soil. These projects will help you know more about soil.

Plant the same kind of seed in two different types of soil.

Place some soil in a flat box like this and set the box out in the yard. After two weeks look at the soil and see what has happened.

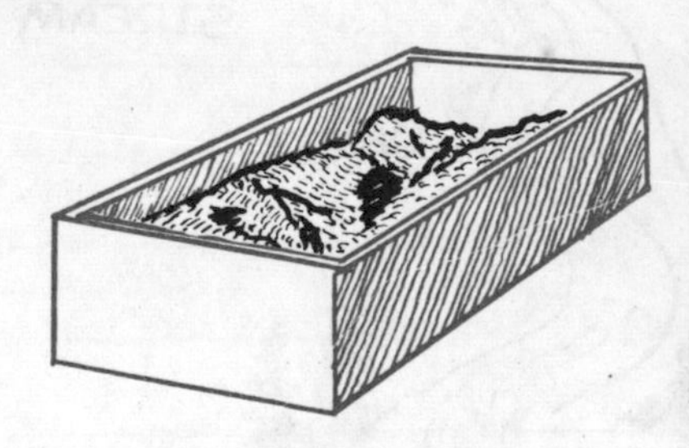

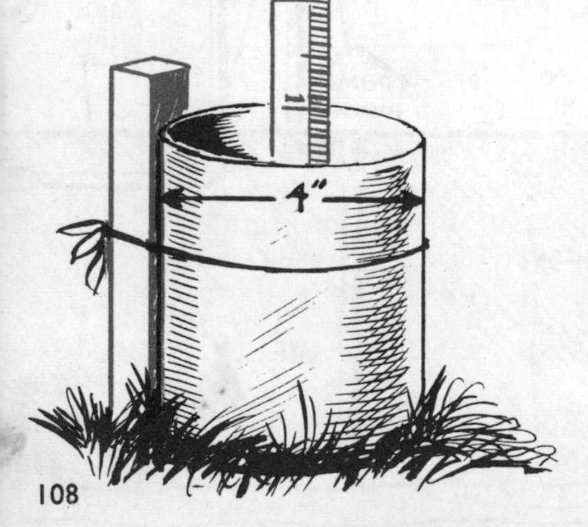

RAIN GAUGE made from a tin can and a ruler.

OUTDOOR CHEF

ELECTIVE 19

Each time you do one of the following things you receive *one credit:*

1. Fix your own supper with at least one hot dish: boiled eggs, hot cereal, boiled rice, spaghetti, stew, potatoes—baked, boiled or fried. Wash and put away the dishes.
2. Help prepare and cook any two of the above dishes outdoors.
3. While on a family picnic help cook part of the meal.

MOTHER'S OR DAD'S INITIALS AND DATE FOR EACH CREDIT

1 V.R.C - 5-8-58

If you cook in the outdoors, this is the time to make some stew. Then you and your family can spend a Saturday afternoon cooking in the backyard. If you do it carefully, it will be the best stew you ever tasted because things certainly taste good when they are cooked outdoors.

FRYING AN EGG

This is something to try in your backyard. The inside of your pan should first be well greased with the natural grease left from frying bacon, or with kitchen fat or butter. Crack the egg gently on the side of the pan and break it apart—just a few inches above the pan so the yolk will not break.

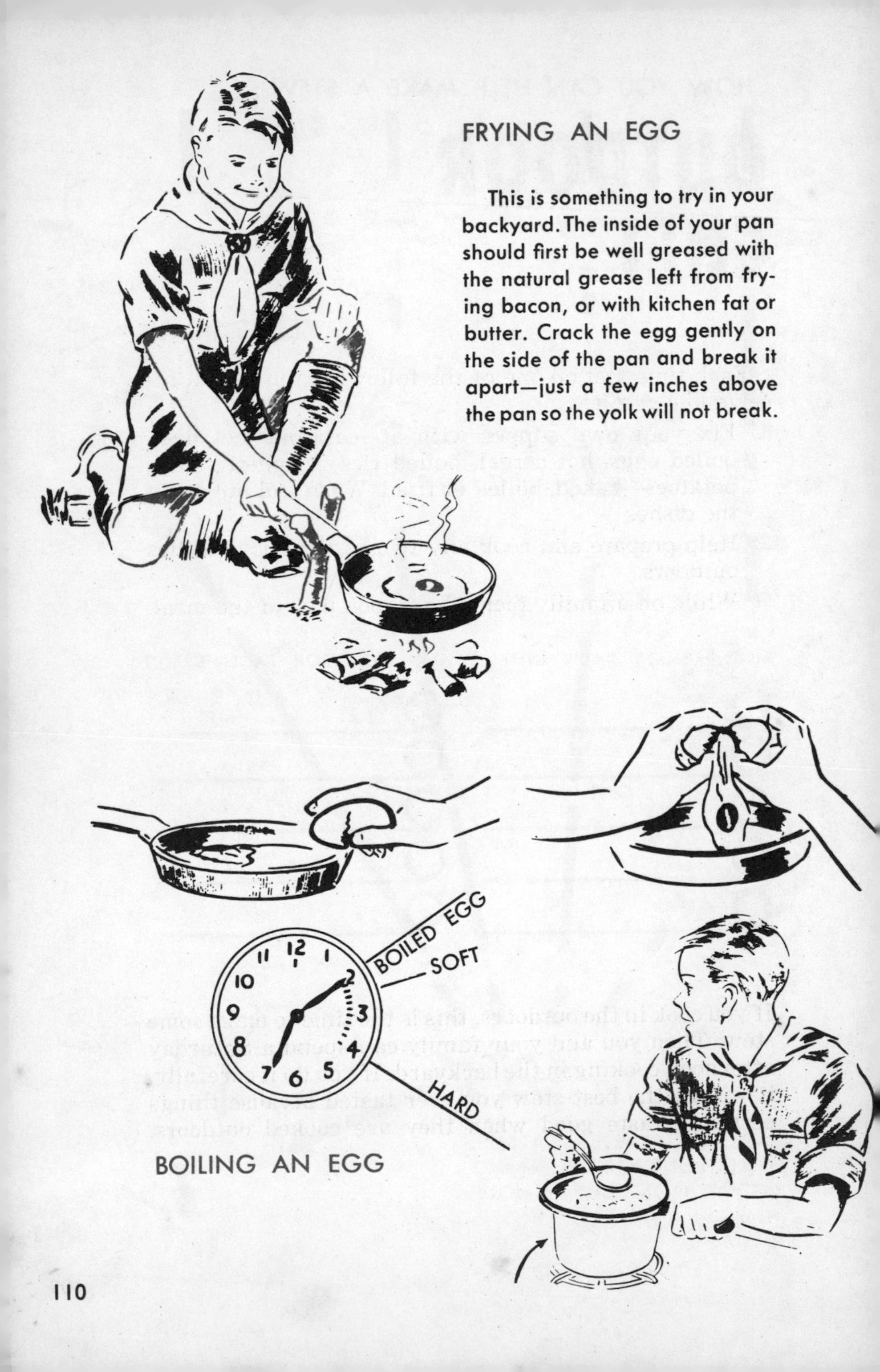

BOILING AN EGG

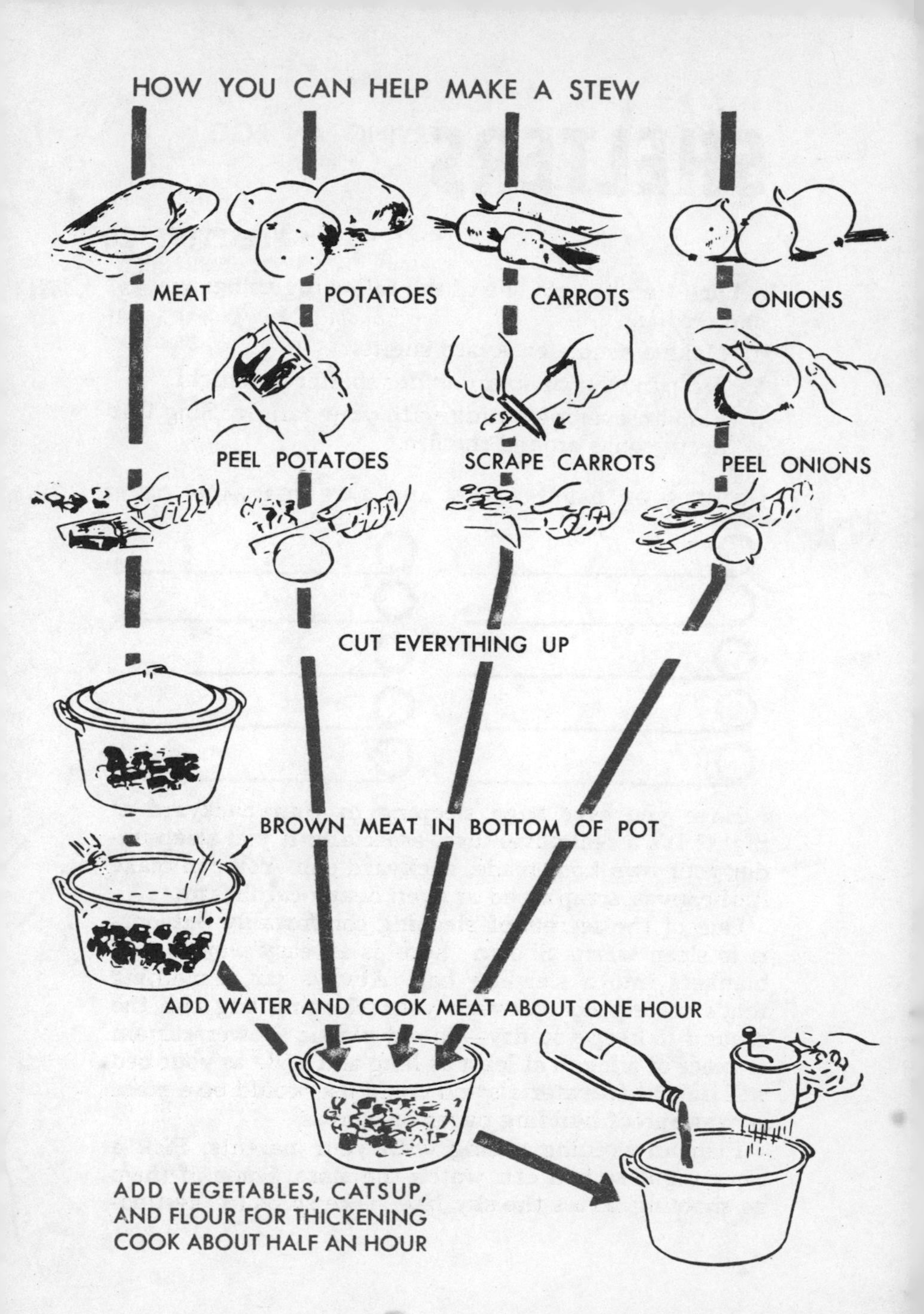
HOW YOU CAN HELP MAKE A STEW
MEAT
POTATOES
CARROTS
ONIONS
PEEL POTATOES
SCRAPE CARROTS
PEEL ONIONS
CUT EVERYTHING UP
BROWN MEAT IN BOTTOM OF POT
ADD WATER AND COOK MEAT ABOUT ONE HOUR
ADD VEGETABLES, CATSUP,
AND FLOUR FOR THICKENING
COOK ABOUT HALF AN HOUR

SHELTERS

ELECTIVE 20

Each time you do one of the following things you get *one credit:*

1. Make a simple backyard shelter.
2. Sleep in your backyard under shelter overnight.
3. Plan an evening outing with your family. Sing Cub Scout songs around the fire.

MOTHER'S OR DAD'S INITIALS AND DATE FOR EACH CREDIT

Have you ever tried sleeping in your backyard at night? It's a real adventure, especially if you sleep under your own homemade, backyard den. You can make it of canvas, scrap wood or even heavy cardboard.

One of the secrets of sleeping comfortably outdoors is to sleep warm. Shown here is an easy way to fold blankets into a sleeping bag. Always put something that's waterproof between your sleeping bag and the ground to keep you dry—an old plastic shower curtain or piece of oilcloth at least as long and wide as your bed will do. Other materials you could use would be a piece of waterproof building paper or canvas.

Plan an evening outing with your parents. Pick a clear night so you can watch the stars. Some of them go shooting across the sky like space ships to "destina-

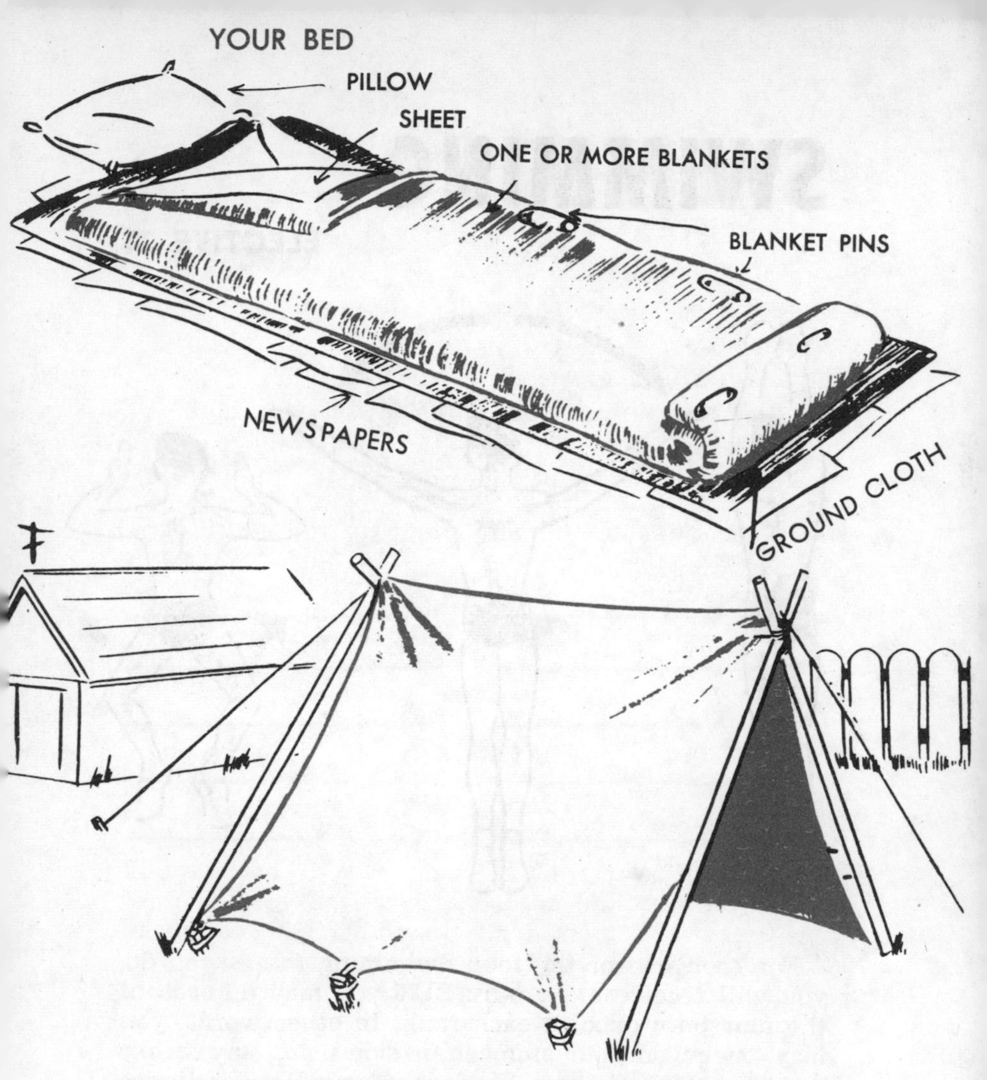

tion unknown." Have mother and dad point out their favorite stars. Maybe you'll be lucky enough to see the northern lights, swinging their mysterious rays across the heavens.

Anyway, take plenty to eat, play a few games after your picnic supper, then sit around the fire and sing songs till it's star study time.

SWIMMING

ELECTIVE 21

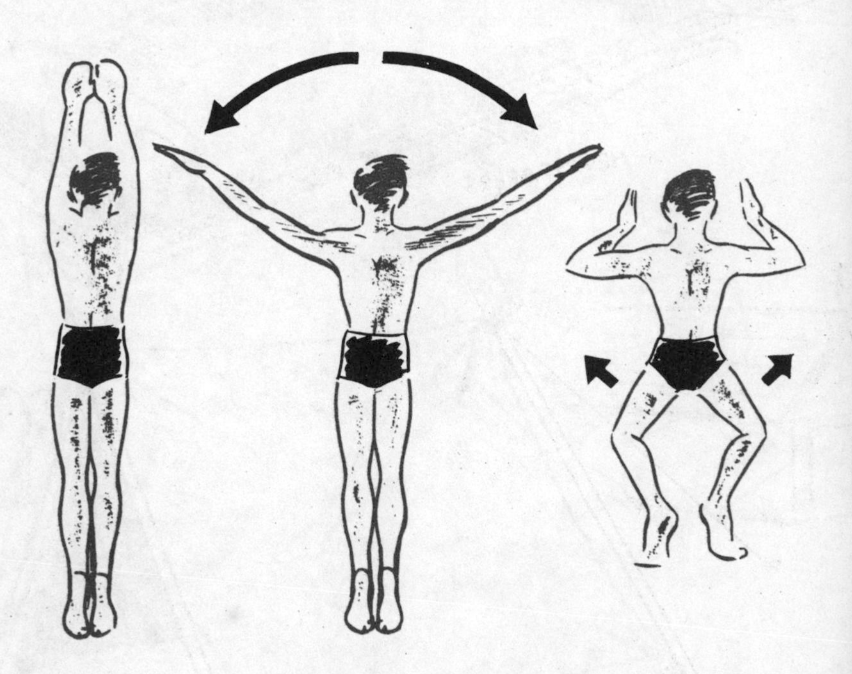

For each one of the four Swimming things you do, you will receive one credit. BUT you may do each of the four only once in each rank. In other words, you may "swim on your stomach or side using any stroke you choose," once as a Wolf, once as a Bear and once as a Lion. The same is true with each of the other three things.

Whenever you are working on your Swimming elective, be sure that you always have an adult who can swim with you.

BREAST STROKE

Practice the arm movement first, standing in water about shoulder deep. Extend your arms straight in front of you. Turn your palms outward and pull to the side and straight back with power. This tends to lift you upwards and forward, at which time you should breathe in through the mouth. The rest of the

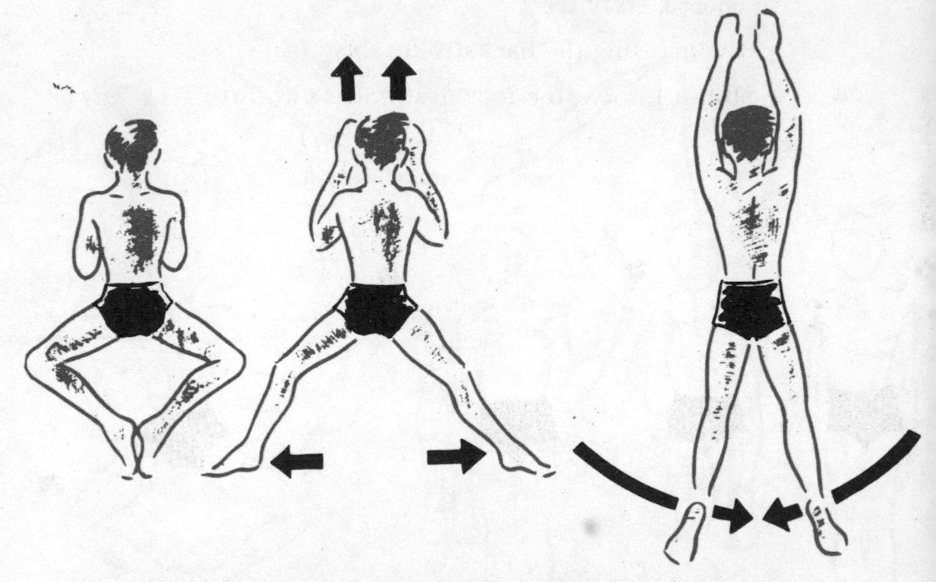

time you should be face down in the water. Next bring your arms in to your sides as shown, then shoot them out straight ahead again for the next stroke.

Practice the leg movement while holding on to the side of the pool or a buoy. With your legs first straight out behind you, draw your knees forward and to the side (not under you), heels together. Then comes the kick. Turn your toes out and kick outward to the side and back.

When you can do both arm and leg movements well, try them together as shown in the pictures—first the arm movement and then, as you finish that, begin the leg movement. Be sure to glide at the end of each kick.

You may receive one credit for doing each of the following things, *but you may earn a credit in each only once in each rank.*

1. Float in water without touching bottom, remaining as motionless as possible, for five minutes.
2. Swim on stomach or side, using any stroke you choose, sixty feet.
3. Swim, using the backstroke, sixty feet.
4. Jump into water feet first and swim fifty feet, any style.

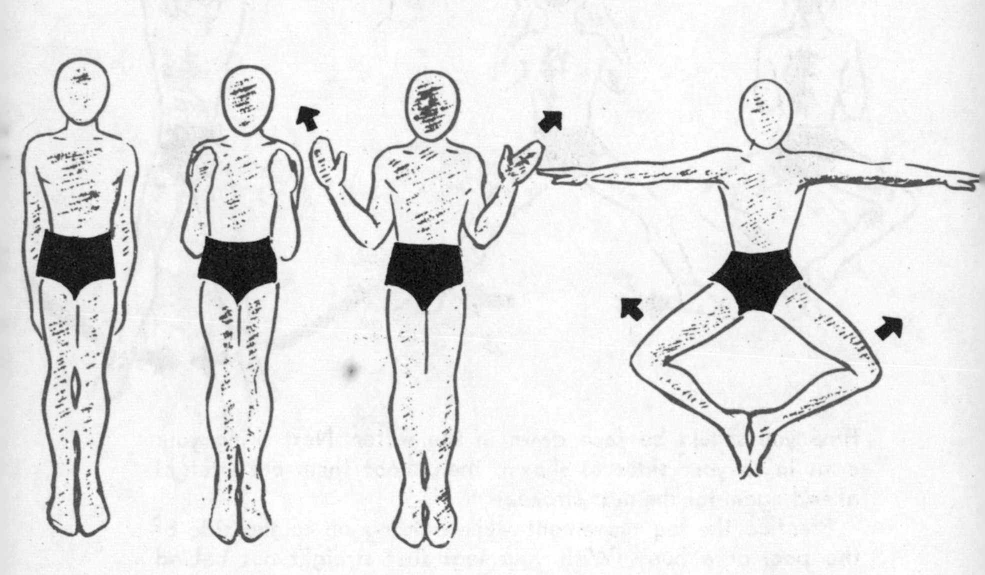

BACK STROKE

Begin by floating on your back, arms down to your sides. Bring your hands up over your chest to your shoulders. Reach straight outward and a little behind. Then pull your arms back to the side with force. At the same time you are beginning the arm

MOTHER'S OR DAD'S INITIALS AND DATE FOR EACH CREDIT

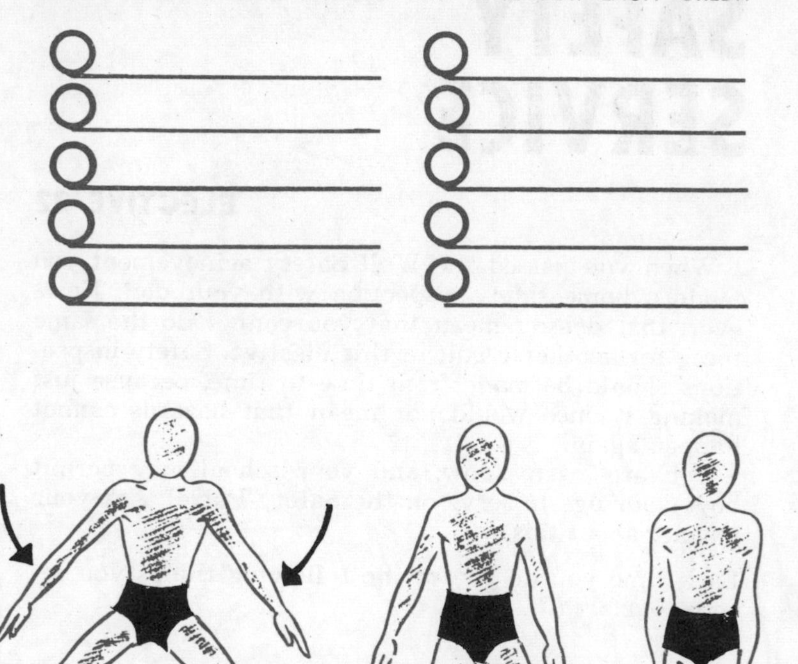

movement, draw your knees back sideward, keeping your feet together. Then spread your legs wide to the sides (just as your arm pull begins) and snap them together to the starting position. Breathe in through your mouth just before each stroke.

SAFETY SERVICE

ELECTIVE 22

When you passed the Wolf Safety achievement you made a home safety inspection with your dad. However, that doesn't mean that you cannot do the same thing for another credit in this elective. Safety inspections should be made from time to time, because just making it once would not mean that hazards cannot happen again.

You are ten now, and your school may permit boys your age to serve on the Safety Patrol. Ask your teacher about this.

Each time you do one of the following things you receive *one credit*.

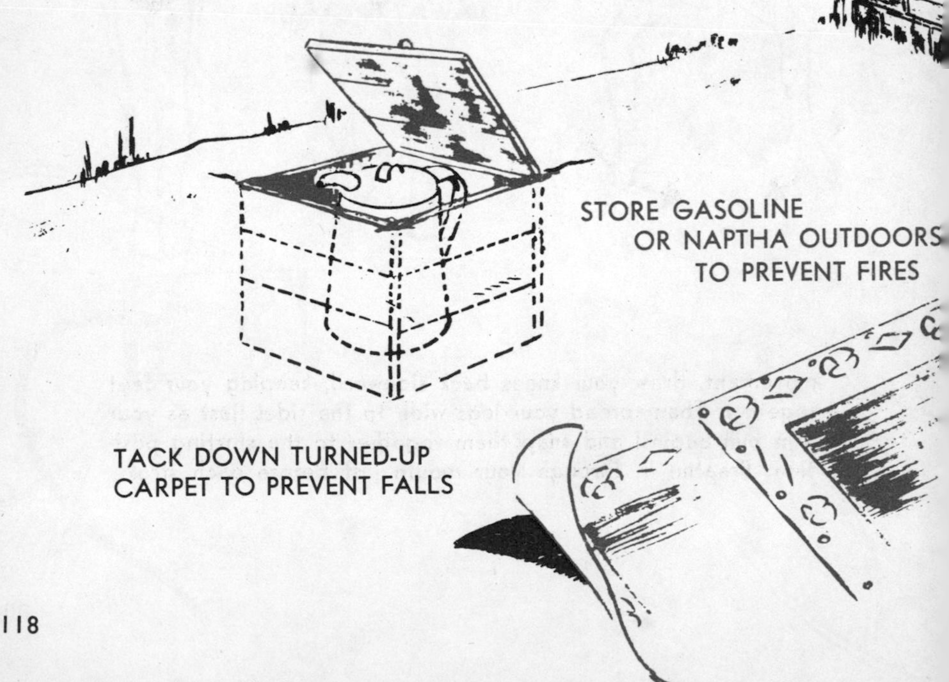

1. If boys your age are permitted, serve on the Safety Patrol in your school for two months while you are a Lion.
2. Inspect your home and, with dad, fix up unsafe conditions.

MOTHER'S OR DAD'S INITIALS AND DATE FOR EACH CREDIT

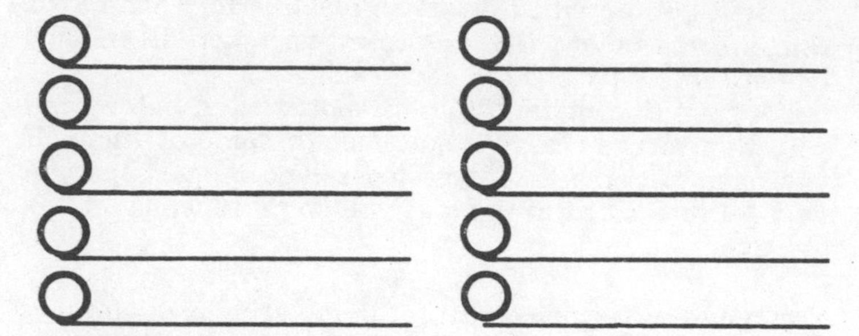

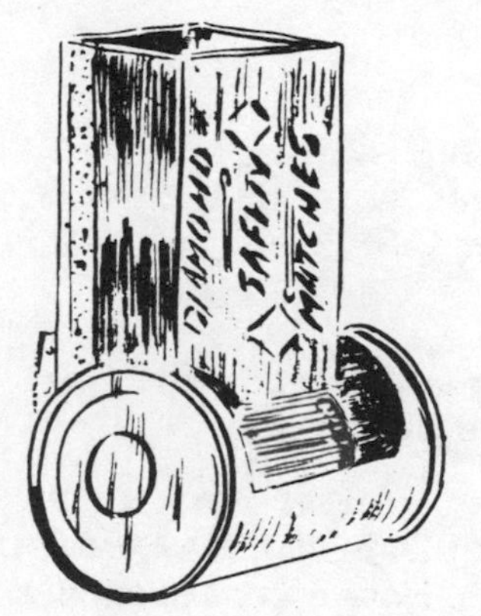

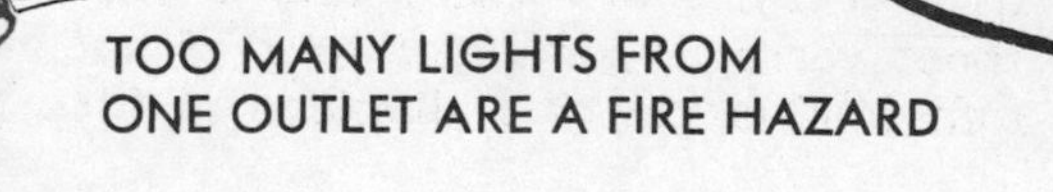

SPORTS

ELECTIVE 23

Before you get interested in this elective, read the rule at the top of the requirements. It tells you that you will get a credit toward an elective for each of the things listed below. BUT you may earn a credit in each one of these only once in each rank.

You will find many different sports listed below, and you may already have done a lot in some of them. If you have never been interested in sports, perhaps you will get interested in them as you begin to work on this elective.

You may receive one credit for doing each of the following things, *but you may earn a credit in each only once in each rank.*

1. In tennis, demonstrate serving, scoring and fault rules for singles. Play a set with dad, mother, brother, Den Chief or another Cub Scout.

2. In baseball, show that you can play at least three positions and take part in two full games.

3. Boating. (Know how to swim.) Demonstrate forward strokes, turn and backstrokes. Row a boat around a 150-yard course set by your dad. Always have some adult with you.

4. In archery, know the safety rules. Know how to shoot correctly, and put four of six arrows into a four-foot target at a distance of fifty feet.

MOTHER'S OR DAD'S INITIALS AND DATE FOR EACH CREDIT

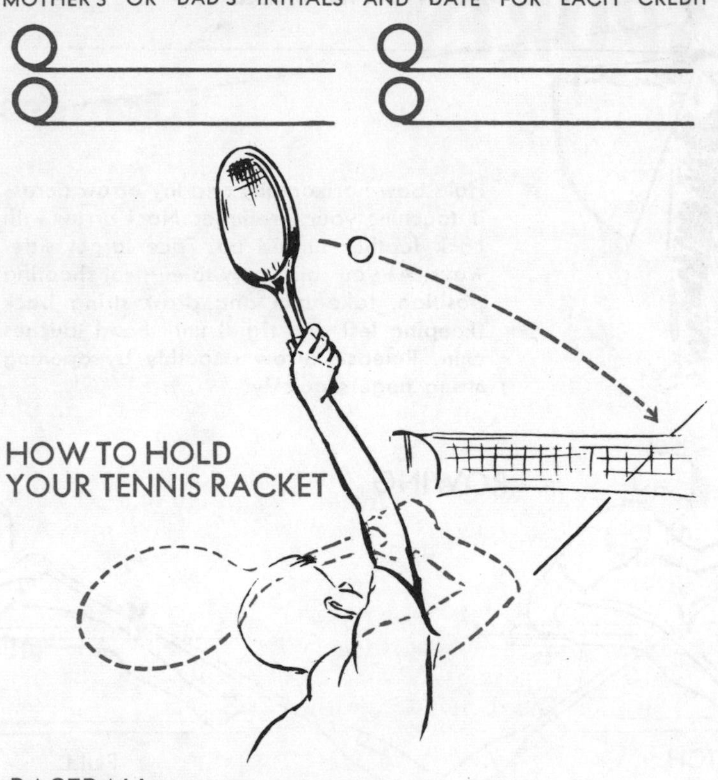

HOW TO HOLD YOUR TENNIS RACKET

BASEBALL

Every American boy knows how to play baseball, so this should be an easy elective credit. If you want to play first base, you have to be able to field hot grounders, bunts, pop flies and fouls. You also have to have a good reach to get high, low and wide throws from infield.

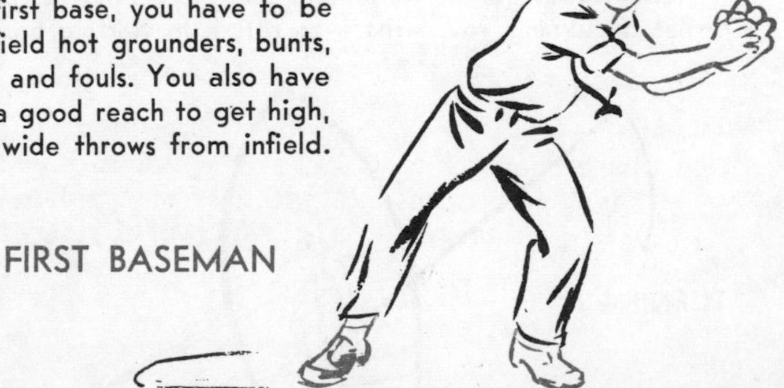

FIRST BASEMAN

HOW TO SHOOT WITH BOW AND ARROW

Hold bow horizontally and lay arrow across it, touching your forefinger. Nock arrow with cock feather turned up. Face target sideways. As you raise bow to vertical shooting position, take aim and draw string back (keeping left arm rigid) until hand touches chin. Release arrow smoothly by opening string fingers quickly.

ROWING

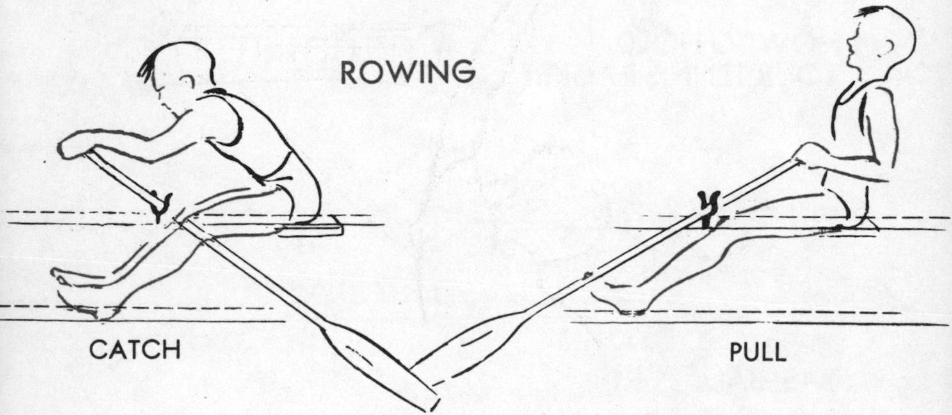

Lean well forward and "catch" your oars by dipping the blades into the water. Pull backward with power of your whole body. Raise blades out of water and "feather"—that is, turn blades flat by turning your wrists—to return to starting position.

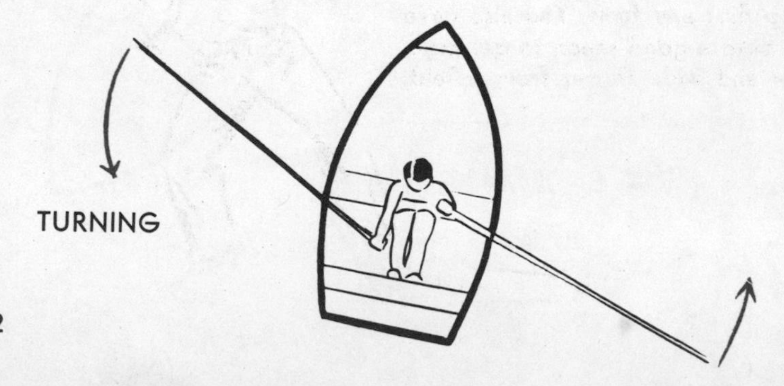

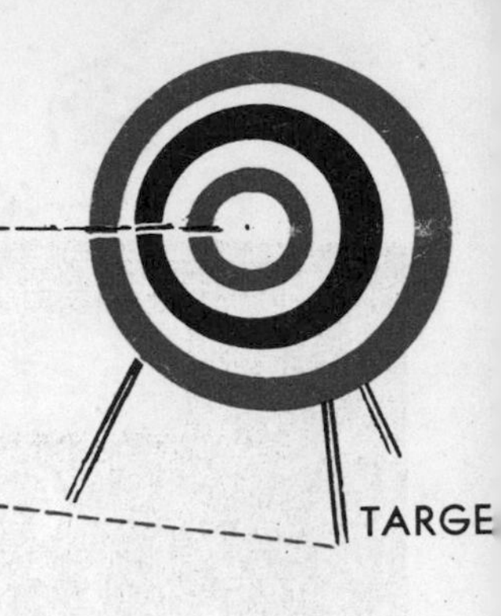

SAFETY RULES

1. Always wear arm guard and finger tab when you shoot.
2. Never nock an arrow until you are ready to shoot.
3. Never aim an arrow at anyone.
4. Shoot only where you have a clear view of the area around target.

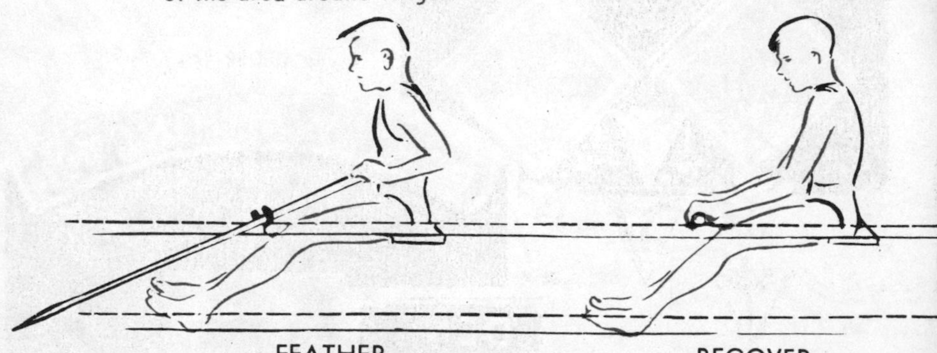

To turn, pull on one oar while simply holding the other blade in the water (as a pivot) or pushing on it in opposite direction, as shown.

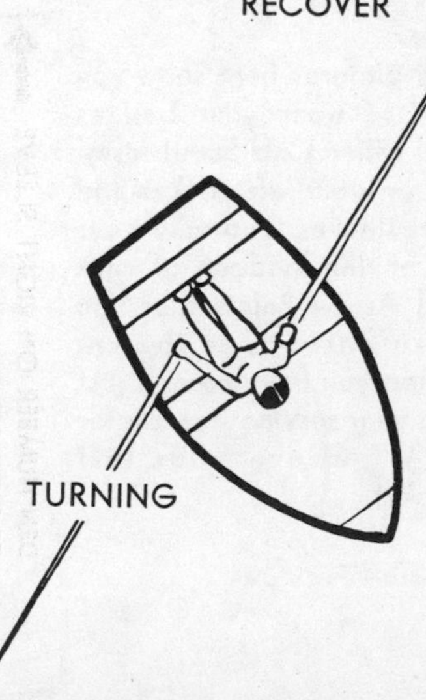

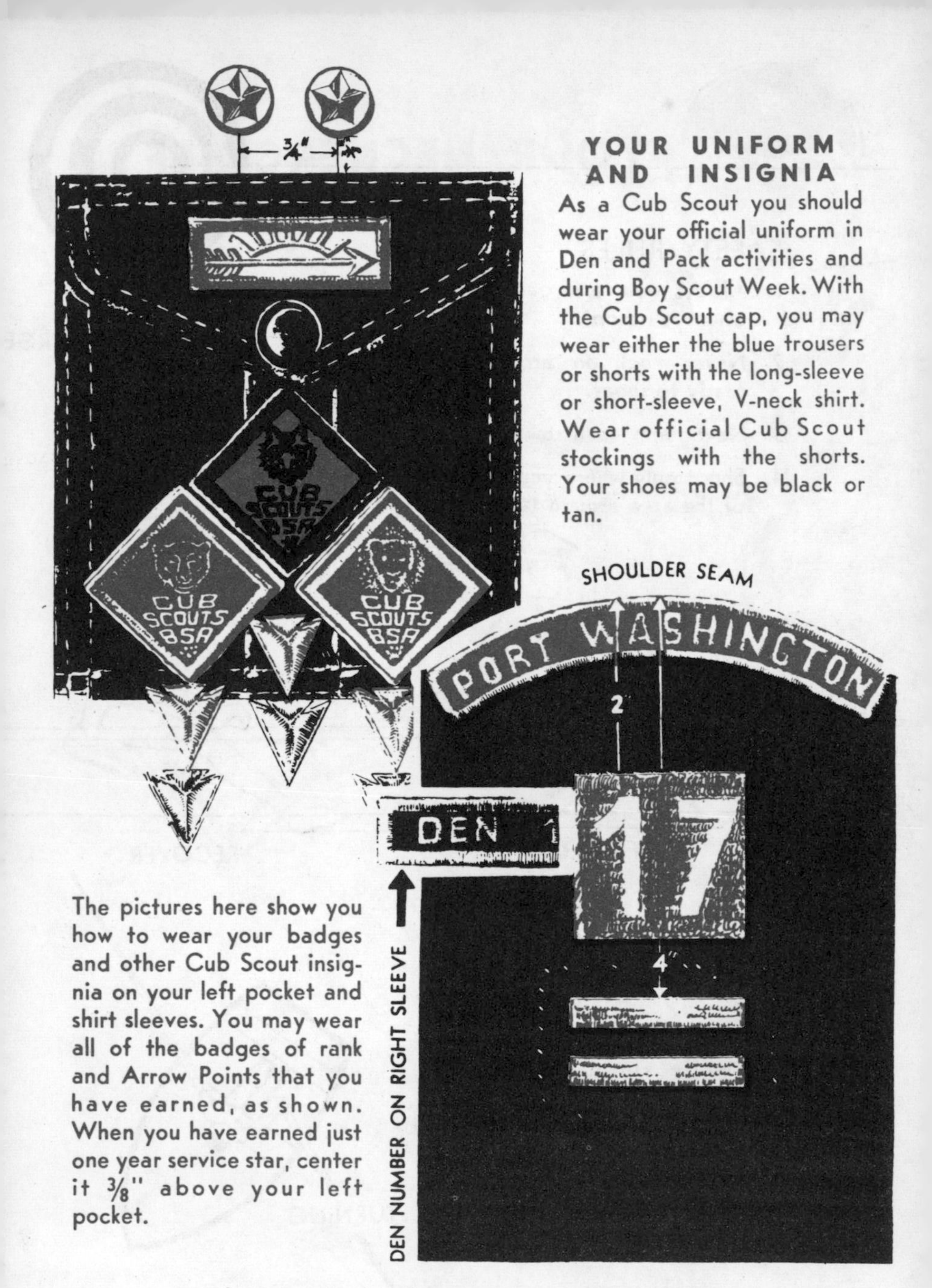

YOUR UNIFORM AND INSIGNIA

As a Cub Scout you should wear your official uniform in Den and Pack activities and during Boy Scout Week. With the Cub Scout cap, you may wear either the blue trousers or shorts with the long-sleeve or short-sleeve, V-neck shirt. Wear official Cub Scout stockings with the shorts. Your shoes may be black or tan.

The pictures here show you how to wear your badges and other Cub Scout insignia on your left pocket and shirt sleeves. You may wear all of the badges of rank and Arrow Points that you have earned, as shown. When you have earned just one year service star, center it 3/8" above your left pocket.

YOUR NECKERCHIEF

(a) Roll long edge over upon itself in several flat folds to about 6" from tip of neckerchief.
(b) Place around neck of V-neck shirt or over collar of official long-sleeved shirt. (The collar of a long-sleeved shirt may be turned under when wearing the neckerchief.)
(c) Draw neckerchief slide over ends and adjust to fit snugly.
(d) Tie ends in a SLIP-KNOT for final smart appearance.

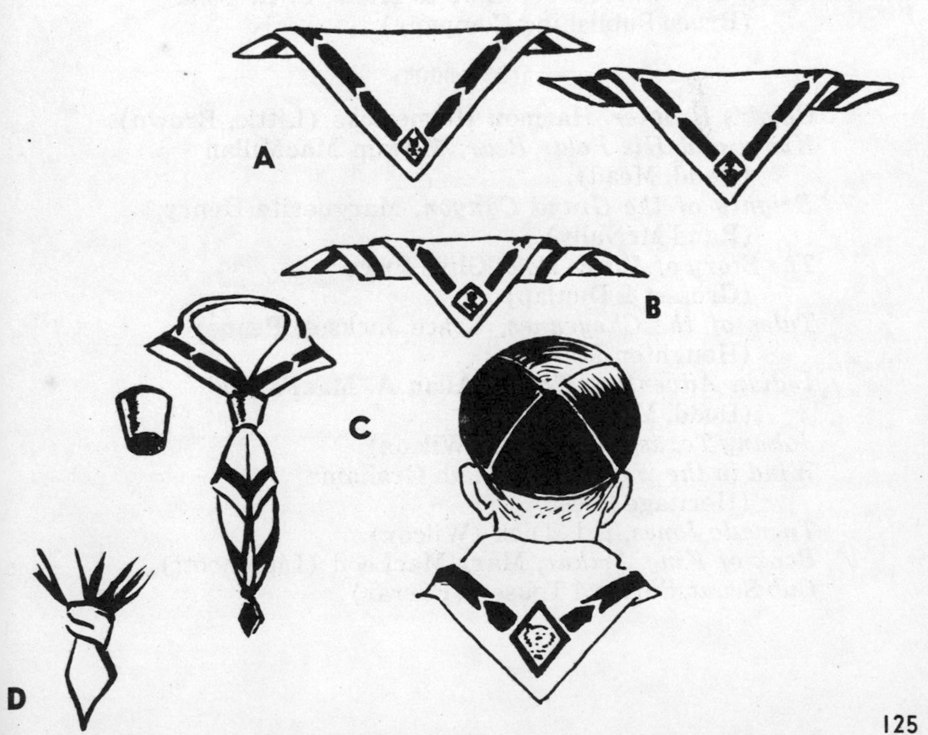

BOOKS FOR CUB SCOUTS

THINGS TO MAKE

Make-It Book (Simon and Schuster).
Boats, Airplanes, Kites, A. J. La Berge (Manual Arts Press).
Child's Book of Carpentry, Jeanne Taylor (Greenberg).
Easy Puppets, Gertrude Pels (Crowell).
Woodcarving as a Hobby, H. W. Faulkner (Harper).
Model Jets and Rockets for Boys, R. F. Yates (Harper).
Airplane Model Building, Gene Johnson (Cornell Maritime Press).
New Tin Can Projects, J. J. Lukowitz (Bruce Publishing Company).
Make It Yourself, B. W. Carlson (Abingdon).
Electrical Things Boys Like to Make, S. R. Cook (Bruce Publishing Company).

STORY BOOKS

Oolak's Brother, Harmon Helmericks (Little, Brown).
Kudla and His Polar Bear, Miriam MacMillan (Dodd, Mead).
Brighty of the Grand Canyon, Marguerite Henry (Rand McNally).
The Story of Marco Polo, Olive Price (Grosset & Dunlap).
Tales of the Cheyennes, Grace Jackson Penney (Houghton-Mifflin).
Indian Adventure Trails, Allan A. MacFarlan (Dodd, Mead).
Johnny Texas, Carol Hoff (Wilcox).
Wind in the Willows, Kenneth Grahame (Heritage Press).
Tornado Jones, T. L. Dick (Wilcox).
Book of King Arthur, Mary MacLeod (Lippincott).
Cub Scout, Sanford Tousey (Farrar).

THINGS TO DO

Mr. Wizard's Science Secrets, Don Herbert (Popular Mechanics Press).
Practical Magic, David Robbins (Greenberg).
Fun for Young Collectors, Joseph Leeming (Lippincott).
Cowboy Jamboree: Western Songs and Lore, H. W. Felton (Knopf).
First Book About Fishing, Steven Schneider (Watts).
Junior Party Book, B. W. Carlson (Abingdon).
Fun in the Water, T. K. Cureton (Assn. Press).
Stampography, R. V. Masters (Sterling).
Coinometry, R. V. Masters & Fred Reinfeld (Sterling).
Photography for Boys and Girls, S. W. Bowler (Crowell).

NATURE AND GARDENING

The Book of Nature Hobbies, Ted Pettit (Didier).
The First Book of Plants, Alice Dickinson (Watts).
Al Alligator, Mac Mallard, Willie Whitetail, Woody Woodchuck, R. W. Eschmeyer (Fisherman Press), Oxford, Ohio.
Oliver Becomes a Weatherman, Jack Bechdolt (Messner).
First Book of Stones, M. B. Cormack (Watts).
Introduction to Wild Flowers, John Kieran (Garden City).
Introduction to Birds, John Kieran (Garden City).
Teach Your Dog New Tricks, Shondell, Tate & Trempe (McGraw).
Picture Book of Insects, A. T. Gaul (Lothrop).
First Book of Snakes, John Hoke (Watts).

ABOUT BOY SCOUTS AND SCOUTING

Boys' Life Book of Scout Stories (Doubleday).
Handbook for Boys (Boy Scouts of America).
The Boy Scout Encyclopedia (Rand McNally).

MORE THINGS TO DO

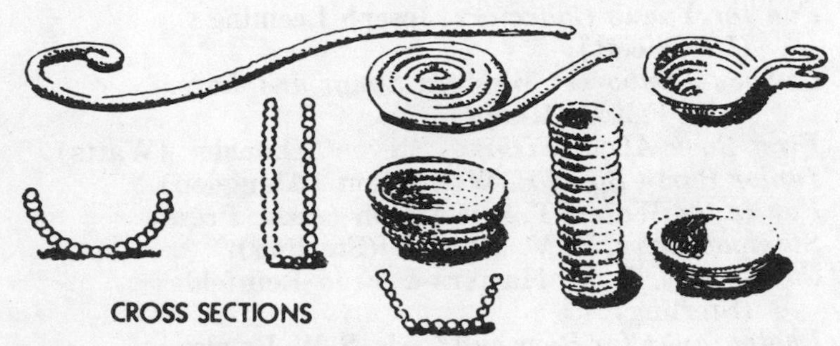

PLASTELINE

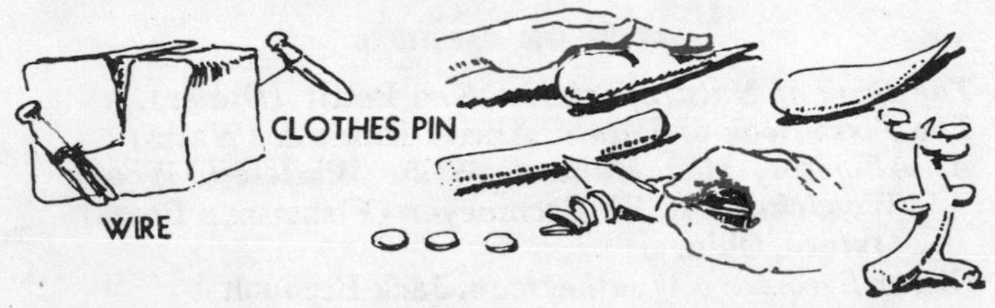

Ready-prepared clay or Plasteline may be bought at an art or potter's supply store. If you use ordinary clay, mix it with water until it feels like thick cream and is free of lumps. Let it dry until it becomes a thick paste before you use it.

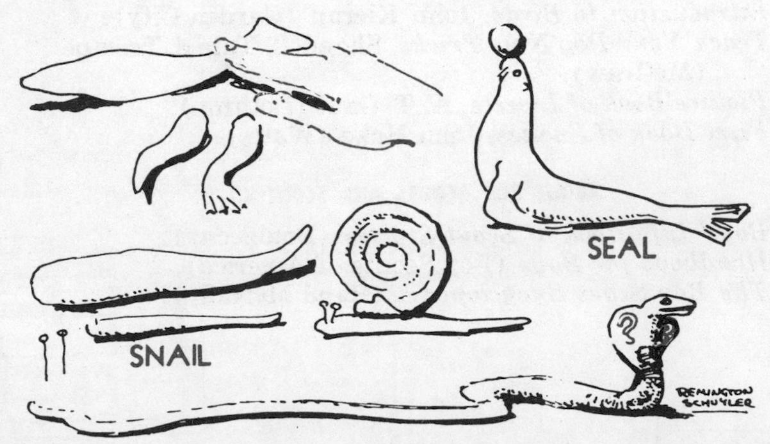

WOODWORKING

SEATS FOR THE DEN

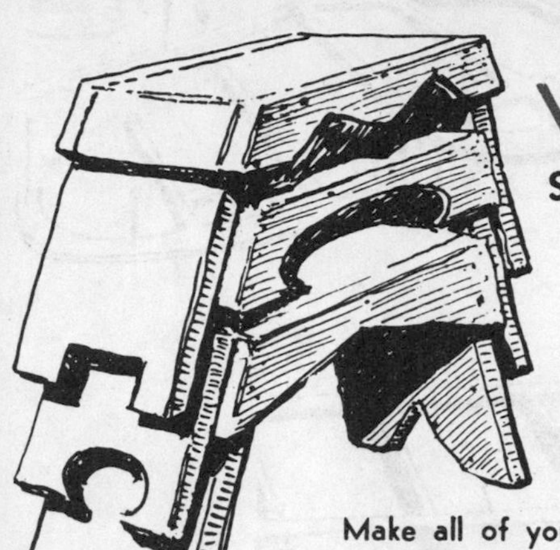

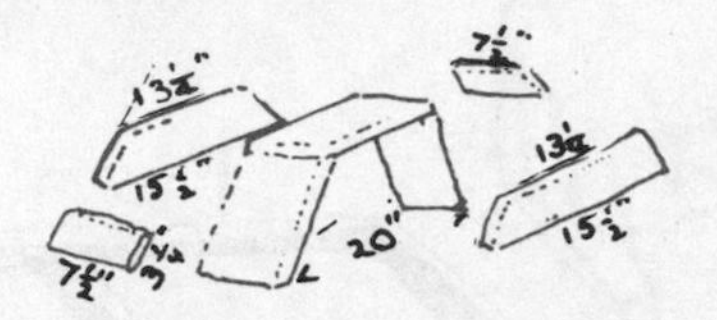

Make all of your benches the same size and they will nest together like this. You will need five feet of board ¾" thick and 7½" wide for each bench. Cut out parts of the sizes shown and nail together.

CEREMONIAL LOG

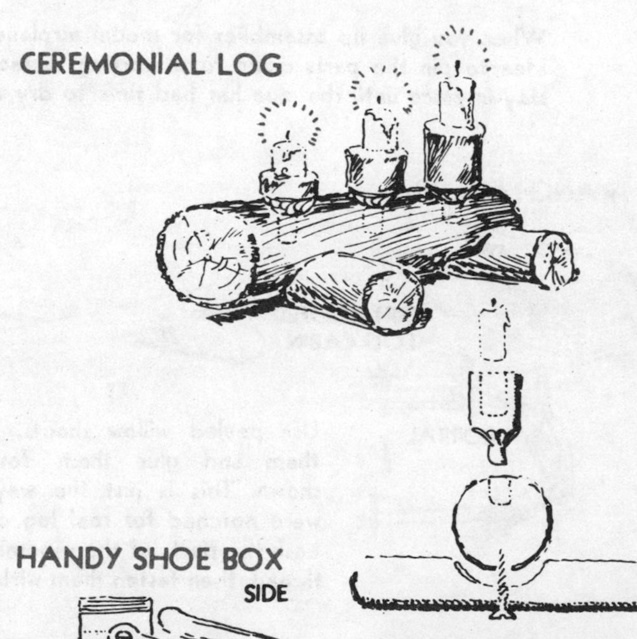

HANDY SHOE BOX

FRONT

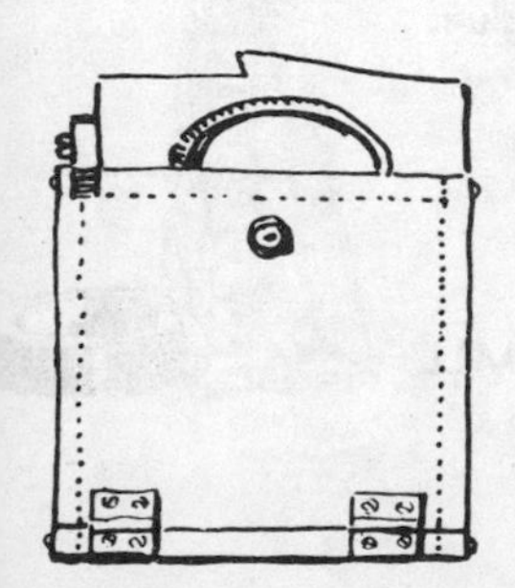

SIDE

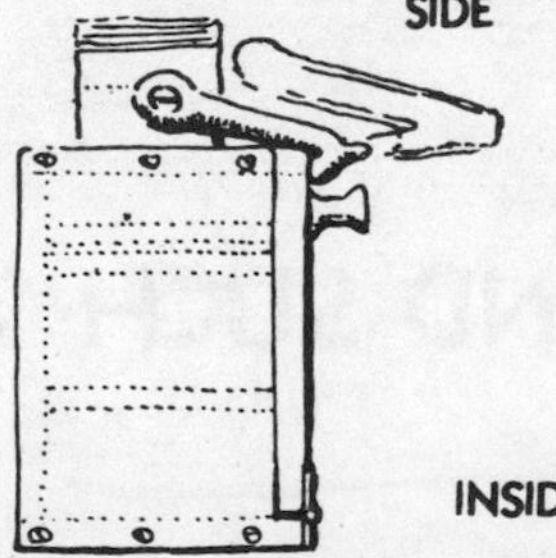

INSIDE

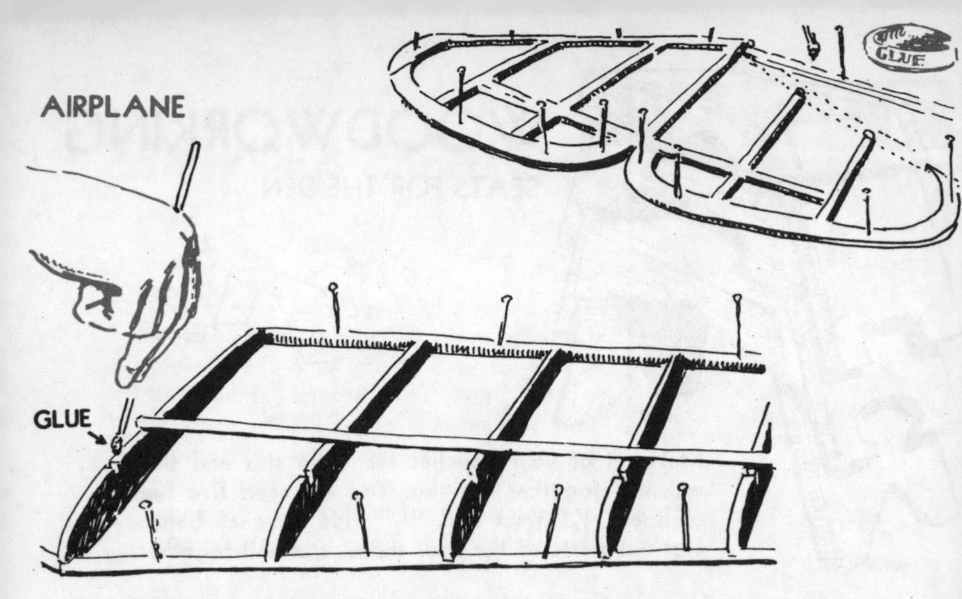

When you glue up assemblies for model airplanes, it's a good idea to pin the parts down to a working surface so they will stay in place until the glue has had time to dry thoroughly.

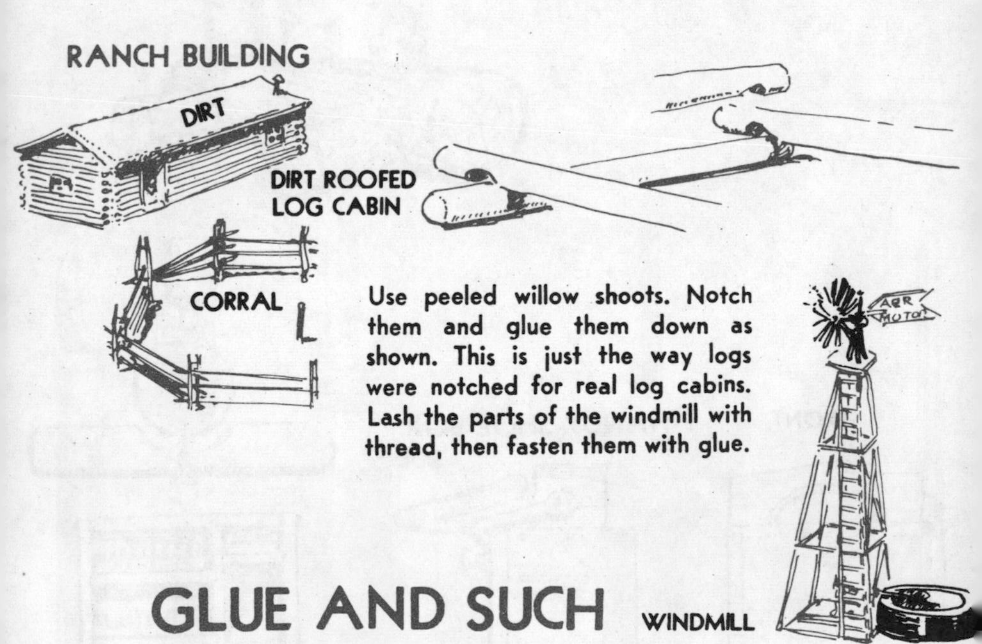

Use peeled willow shoots. Notch them and glue them down as shown. This is just the way logs were notched for real log cabins. Lash the parts of the windmill with thread, then fasten them with glue.

GLUE AND SUCH

WINDMILL

GOUGES & KNIVES

You can easily make your own wood-carving tools as shown here. For a gouge, drive a broken umbrella rib into a hole bored in a broom handle, and then sharpen the edge. Broken hacksaw blades are fine for making carving knives. With these tools, try making printing blocks of linoleum. Carve away the parts that are not to print. Be sure that all letters you carve are in reverse. Glue the piece of linoleum to a wood block for printing.

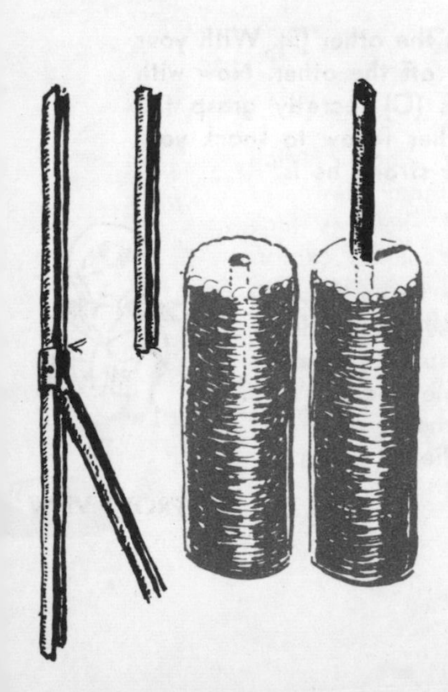

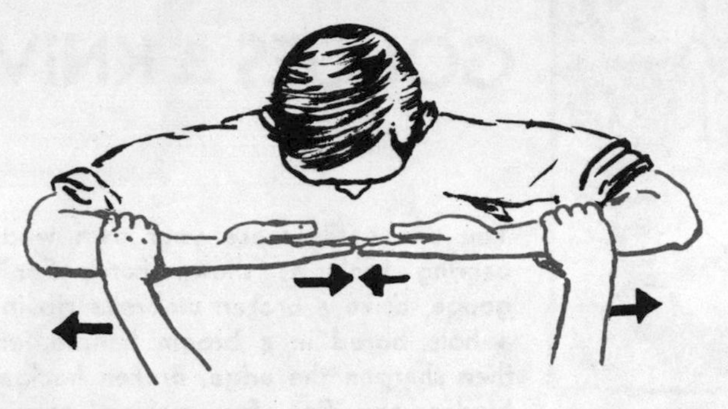

Hold your finger tips like this and challenge another Cub Scout to pull them apart. Looks easy, but try it. You'll be surprised.

TRICKS AND PUZZLES

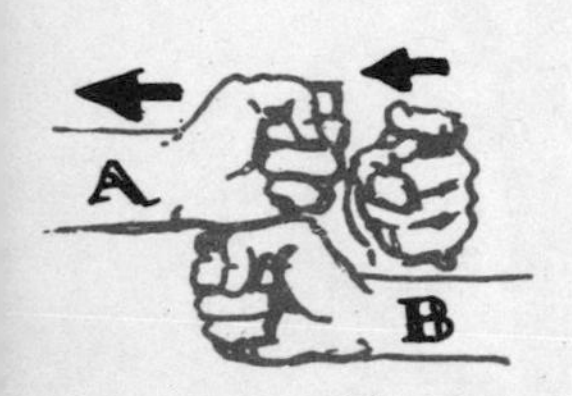

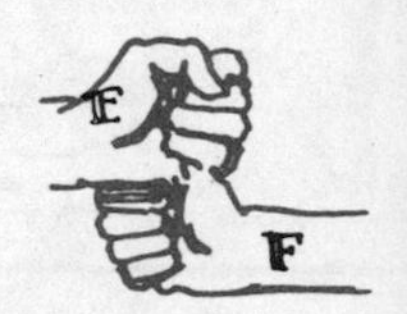

Ask somebody to place one fist (A) on the other (B). With your finger tips it is easy to knock one fist off the other. Now with the palm of one of your own hands (C) secretly grasp the thumb of the other (D). Invite the other fellow to knock your fist off. He can't do it, no matter how strong he is.

SIDE VIEW

Here's a good fun trick for a Pack show. Cub Scout B locks his hands behind his back. Cub Scout A pushes his arms through the hole under B's arms. While B talks, A makes different motions to make audience laugh.

FRONT VIEW

WEBELOS

YOU AND BOY SCO

There once was a boy who lived in a region of farms. He was wild with the love of the outdoors—the trees, the tree-top singers, the wild flowers, and the animals that left their tracks in the mud along the creek banks.

There were other things, too—the migrating flights of wild geese and ducks, sand hill cranes, and other birds that moved in and rested awhile before continuing south for the winter.

He wanted to learn to camp out—to live again the life of his pioneer grandfather who knew the trick of making a home in the wilderness, to learn the ways of the antelope, the nesting habits of birds, and the beauty of the sunsets so vividly described by his mother.

He reveled in the tales of courage and heroic deeds of red men and white as told in *The Deerslayer* and *The Last of the Mohicans*. He longed for the chance to learn tracking and trailing skills, to sleep in the woods, and to climb mountains—to go downstream on a raft like

TING

Huck Finn and Tom Sawyer. He was invited to join a Boy Scout Troop and was asked to buy his first copy of the *Handbook for Boys*. Here at last was the book he had been searching for–a book that would teach him the skills he wanted to know —a book that introduced him to some of the secrets of the four-footed animals, the fish, the snakes, the insects, the birds, the plants and the stars. It guided him not in the way of the scholar or astronomer but in the way of the camper and Scout.

As he grew up he learned that years of experience went into the writing of that book, that many years on the trail in sun and driving rain, sleet and snow, proved that Mother Nature takes care of those who help themselves and is cruel to those who do not.

The deep desire and interest you have for the outdoors can be satisfied during your Boy Scout experience just ahead of you. Do you know that you, too, can experience some of the thrills and skills of your pioneer ancestors?

The term "Scout" means to *look* or *search,* to explore a region or a country, to observe, to watch, to look for, or to follow.

The trained Boy Scout today is an expert in town as well as in the woods, in a canoe in fast water or in a row boat on the lake. He cán take part in swimming, wildlife protection, boating, hiking, pioneering, photography, first aid, camping. He is reverent, trustworthy, loyal, brave, courteous, thrifty, obedient, and kind.

Do you want to have well-developed muscles, a sound body that won't fail you? Do you want to know how to help others, to react naturally and quickly in a time of need? Do you want to know how to swim well enough to save a life besides your own? Do you want to be a "good man" on the trail, an expert camper, an alert tracker?

Do you want to form habits that will make you skillful, self-reliant, observant—habits that will make your life successful? Then no matter where you live, your

place is in a Boy Scout Troop, for you will find in Scouting the activities that will meet your needs and desires. The *Handbook for Boys* is the work of many men, each an expert in his field. It is their best effort to show you the way.

When you get your copy, go over the Tenderfoot requirements with your dad and start immediately learning the skills which will help you become an expert Scout.

On the following pages is a little story about the Boy Scout Troop and how it is organized.

The Troop differs, in some ways, from your Den and Pack. For instance, it is more "grown up"—the way you older fellows want it. More of the leaders are Boy Scouts elected to serve in some office. The Troop doesn't have any Den Mothers because the things you will do as a Boy Scout are skills taught by men or older experienced Boy Scouts and Explorers.

Many Troops have Mothers' Clubs that help the Troop with dinners and things like that.

YOUR NEW UNIFORM

When the Indian boy became older and wiser in the ways of his people, he changed his feathers for a headdress. So you, the Cub Scout, will change yours to the khaki of the Boy Scout—the uniform of the outdoors.

Wear your uniform on all Scouting activities — hiking, camping, rallies, demonstrations, special church services, Boy Scout Week activities, Boards of Review, Courts of Honor, Troop meetings.

You can earn money for your uniform by making and selling handicraft articles, weeding gardens, shoveling snow, mowing lawns, cleaning windows, taking care of a furnace, removing ashes, washing cars, washing dogs, taking care of pets while owners are away, baby sitting, running errands, delivering packages. You can think of lots of other ways, too.

What you can do RIGHT NOW

When you are eleven you can join a *Troop* and be a full-fledged Scout. Right *now* is the time to get ready for that great experience.

If you are ten years and six months old you can start on your Webelos requirements listed on page 146. If you're not, you can complete your Lion achievements. If you are a Lion Cub Scout and still have a month or two to wait before you can start on your Webelos rank, go to work on some electives. We have listed a few on the following pages that will be especially helpful to you as a Boy Scout.

Start on your Webelos as soon as you are old enough. Maybe there are a few other boys in your Pack who are working on their Webelos requirements. Maybe on Saturday all of you could get together and work on some of the requirements together. Your dad or your Den Dad or maybe the Cubmaster will give you fellows a little extra help.

You can qualify for and receive your Webelos badge by the time you are ten years and nine months old. If you do, you will still have time to have some elective fun by doing some of the projects with your dad or mother.

YOUR SCOUTMASTER

The first man you will meet in the Troop will be your Scoutmaster. He is the grown up leader in charge of the Troop and one of the best friends you could possibly have.

He is there to help you when you need help.

Three months before your eleventh birthday you and your dad should visit the Troop and get acquainted with the Scoutmaster.

YOUR PATROL

When you join the Troop you will become a member of a Patrol—your own gang. In a way it's like your Den in the Pack.

In the Patrol you have a little more to say about the things your Troop plans to do. Each Patrol elects one of its own gang to be a Patrol Leader and he serves not only as the leader of the Patrol, but becomes a member of the Patrol Leaders' Council, which helps plan the Troop meetings. Your Patrol Leader tells the Council what his Patrol would like to do, as do the other Patrol Leaders. Together they work out a program which is helpful to all.

Patrols have names, usually that of an animal or bird. They wear a Patrol medallion to identify their members. They also have a Patrol flag which they carry proudly on hikes or fly over their campsite. Pictured here is a Patrol medallion of the Fox Patrol, and a Patrol flag.

Patrols meet once a week and frequently go hiking and camping. You can learn your Scout skills when you're on these trips. You build fires and cook your meals and learn as you go along how to live comfortably and how to take care of yourself in the great outdoors.

Your Patrol Leader is usually an older Scout with experience enough to show you how to get started and how to improve your skill as you go along.

YOUR TROOP

Troops have more than one Patrol. When these Patrols get together it's called a Troop meeting. Most Troops meet once a week.

At your Troop meeting you will have games and ceremonies and practice the things you will do when you go camping or take part in a big community project.

You will learn how to pack your knapsack, how to use a compass and read a map, how to tie useful knots, and how to bandage a wound.

From time to time the Troop will have parties or outings for the families of all Scouts and your mother and dad will be most welcome.

The Troop has several boy leaders who help run it, plus several men, known as Troop Committeemen, who help out when called upon. Perhaps your dad would like to join the Troop Committee. If so, he should tell the Scoutmaster he's willing to help out.

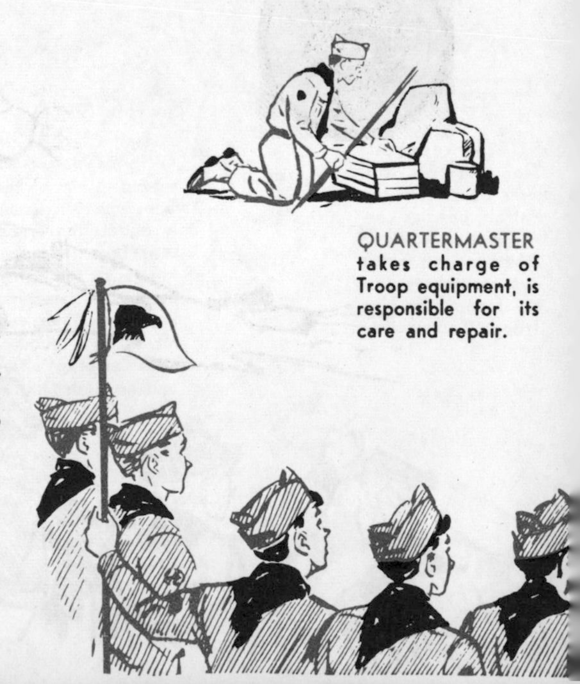

QUARTERMASTER takes charge of Troop equipment, is responsible for its care and repair.

THE DEN CHIEF IS ALSO A TROOP OFFICER He helps Cub Scouts prepare for their Boy Scout experience. Maybe after you've been in the Troop a while you will want to earn your Den Chief's Cord by helping out in your old Pack.

THE SPONSOR Your church, synagogue, P.T.A. or some other group sponsors your Troop.

YOUR TROOP COMMITTEE picks a suitable meeting place and appoints the Scoutmaster and his Assistants.

YOUR SCOUTMASTER is the key man in your Troop. He leads through example and encouragement.

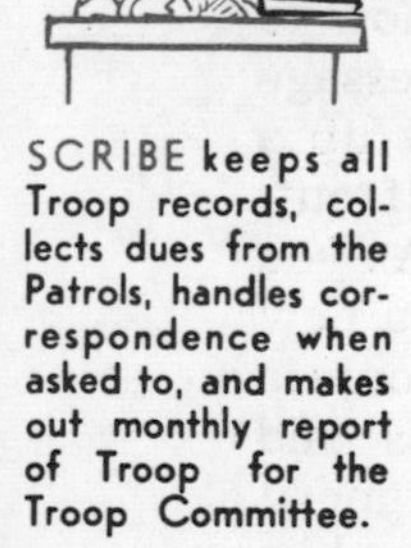

SCRIBE keeps all Troop records, collects dues from the Patrols, handles correspondence when asked to, and makes out monthly report of Troop for the Troop Committee.

SENIOR PATROL LEADER A First Class Scout. Performs duties assigned to him by the Scoutmaster. Usually directs the Troop meeting program. He assists the Patrol Leaders in planning Patrol meetings and hikes and encourages Patrol activities and advancement.

ASSISTANT SCOUTMASTERS help your Scoutmaster out in any way he directs — with hikes, camping trips, advancement or other special jobs.

JUNIOR ASSISTANT SCOUTMASTERS are Explorers of at least 15 years of age who serve the Troop as experts in first aid, signalling or other special assignment.

YOUR PATROL LEADER is the leader of his Patrol and a leader in the Troop. He has an Assistant Patrol Leader.

A NEW LADDER TO CLIMB

Boy Scout advancement is filled with many new things to do—how to splice rope, how to signal a message with flags or lights, how to set up a camp and take care of yourself outdoors in all kinds of weather. As you do these things you will climb a new ladder of ranks. First you become a Tenderfoot, then Second Class and First Class. After that there are merit badges in all kinds of things boys like to make and do. These lead to Star, Life and—the highest rank of all—Eagle.

YOUR NEW ADVANCEMENT

Your advancement in the Troop will come about in a little different way from the way it did in the Pack.

In Cub Scouting, remember, you passed all achievements to your mother or dad. But in Boy Scouting you will be completing requirements out on the trail, in camp, in many places where your parents aren't present. Remember, too, that you are learning *man* skills now, skills that will make you self-reliant and resourceful. You will be taught by your Patrol Leader and other leaders. For your Tenderfoot rank you will be reviewed by your Scoutmaster, and when he is satisfied that you know the requirements you will be invested as a Tenderfoot Scout with a ceremony at the Troop meeting.

BOARD OF REVIEW

In the Troop you will find that they hold a Board of Review, usually once a month, where you have a chance to be reviewed on your Second or First Class rank.

The Board of Review is a meeting of the Troop Committee, some of whom are dads. They sit around a table and talk with you about what you did when you built your fire for Second Class cooking, or what the Scout Oath and Law mean to you. They aren't trying to "catch" you in anything; they just want to be sure you understand what you know about the requirements.

COURT OF HONOR

The Court of Honor is usually a special feature at a Troop meeting where all badges earned are awarded. It's really something special. Sometimes it's held outdoors around a campfire.

W·E·B·E·L·O·S REQUIREMENTS

Your last step in Cub Scouting is one that gets you all set to be a Boy Scout. This step is the Webelos rank, the highest rank in Cub Scouting. When you are ready to pass your Webelos requirements, go to your Cubmaster and pass them directly to him.

Here are the requirements you must meet:

1. You must be at least ten and one-half years old. You may start to earn your Webelos badge any time after you are ten and one-half years of age.

2. You must be a Lion Cub Scout. If you are ten and just joining the Cub Scouts, you can earn your Lion badge by first becoming a Wolf and then a Bear. Or, you may earn your Lion badge by starting immediately on your Lion achievements.

3. Show that you are prepared in the Tenderfoot Scout requirements as given in the *Handbook for Boys.* You will actually pass these requirements to your Scoutmaster when you join a Troop.

Your Boy Scout Tenderfoot requirements are the things you should be able to do by the time you become a Boy Scout. Your Den Chief can help you learn these.

4. Show that you are ready to become a Boy Scout by choosing one of the following:
   A. A home service project. (Choose it with the help of your parents.)

   OR

   B. A Den service project. (Choose it with the help of your Den Mother.)

   OR

   C. Pack or chartered institution project. (Choose it with the help of your Cubmaster.)

   Do your best to carry out this service project for a period of two months or for a shorter period of time if you do not have two months remaining before you are eleven.

   If you do a home service project, then your mother or dad should sign it. If you do a Den service project, your Den Mother should sign it. If you do a Pack or institution project, your Cubmaster should sign it.

5. Three months before your eleventh birthday, or any time afterwards, visit a meeting of the Troop you wish to join and talk to the Scoutmaster.

   When you visit the Troop meeting, talk to the Scoutmaster about joining. This is important because it gives you a chance to get acquainted with the Scoutmaster and get plans started for your joining the Troop.

6. Three months before your eleventh birthday, or any time afterwards, get an individual Boy Scout membership application form, fill it out, and have your parents sign it. Give it to the Scoutmaster of the Troop you expect to join.

HELPS
ALONG THE WEBELOS TRAIL

The goal of every Cub Scout is to become a Boy Scout—with hiking and camping—and more fun ahead in a Patrol and Troop!

We want to help you meet the six WEBELOS requirements so that you can become a Tenderfoot Scout the very minute you are eleven years old. Becoming a Webelos will guide you to the fun you'll find as a Boy Scout in a Patrol and Troop.

Below are some helps which explain in detail the six WEBELOS requirements.

REQUIREMENTS 1 and 2

Read them again to be sure you're ready to start along the Webelos trail.

REQUIREMENT 3

Show that you are prepared in the Tenderfoot Scout requirements.

To help you do this we list the Tenderfoot requirements as they appear in the *Handbook for Boys*. That is the official Boy Scout handbook:

To become a Tenderfoot Scout you must be at least eleven years of age and do the following:

I. Scout Spirit—Learning about the ideals and traditions of Scouting:

1. Repeat from memory the Scout Oath or Promise and the twelve points of the Scout Law, the Scout Motto and the Scout slogan, and explain the meaning of each in your own words.
2. Describe the Scout badge and explain its meaning. Tell when to wear the Scout uniform and

how to use and care for it.

3. Give the Scout sign, salute and handclasp.

II. Scout Participation—Knowing about the Patrol and Troop, the community and the country of which you are a part:

1. Explain the name of the Patrol you will join and give its call or yell. Tell who your Scout leaders are and what they do in the Troop. Explain, in a general way, what you have to do to become a Second Class and a First Class Scout.
2. Tell how, in an emergency, you would get in contact with the doctor or hospital and with the police or sheriff's office nearest to your home. Explain how, in your community, you would report a fire.
3. Describe the Flag of the United States of America and tell its history in brief. Tell when to fly it. Show how to hoist, lower, display and fold the Flag and how to salute it.

III. Scoutcraft—Setting out to learn a few simple things that all Scouts should know:

1. Tell why it is important to care for a cut or a scratch and show on yourself how to do it. Tie a bandage with a square knot.
2. Explain what care should be taken before building a fire in the open. Describe the harm to a live tree that results from hacking it with an axe or other sharp tool.
3. Whip the ends of a rope at least one-quarter inch in diameter. Join two ropes with a sheet-bend. Attach a rope to a post or rail with a clove hitch, then untie it and fasten it again with two half hitches. Fasten one end of a rope around your waist with a bowline.

When you have met the Tenderfoot requirements before your Scoutmaster (or have been reviewed in the

Cub Scout Webelos requirements by your Scoutmaster) and have proved to him that you thoroughly understand the Scout Oath and Law, you become a Tenderfoot Scout. You will be given your Tenderfoot pin at a ceremony in front of your Patrol and Troop.

REQUIREMENT 4

Before an Indian boy became a "brave", he had to prove himself. He did this by doing some deed which helped those around him.

Before becoming a Boy Scout, you will want to show that you are ready. Choose a service project that will help your home, your Den or your Pack. But first, talk it over with your mother and dad and your Den and Pack leaders.

Some projects are pictured on the following pages. They are only suggestions, though. Perhaps you will decide on another.

Home Service Project — *Choose it with the help of your parents*

Do your best to carry out this service project for a period of two months or for a shorter period of time if you do not have two months remaining before you are eleven.

Do the dishes on a regular night each week—say every Thursday.

Wash certain windows every Saturday morning.

Sit with the baby one night a week.

Set the table and put the chairs up every evening.

Keep your room clean, hang up clothes, make your own bed.

Take complete care of dog or cat.

The purpose of the service project is to show that you can be relied upon to do a job regularly.

We have pictured a few home projects on this page. There are many others. Talk it over with your mother and dad. Find out what you can do that will be helpful.

Helping around the house makes you an important member of the greatest team in the world—your family.

A Den Service Project — *Choose it with the help of your Den Mother*

The Den may need something you can make, the Den Mother may need you to run special errands once each week, or there may be a young Cub Scout who needs some special help to get him started.

Your Den Mother will have several suggestions for you in addition to those pictured on this page. Remember, these are only suggestions, not requirements—so talk it over with her.

Write and distribute notices to Den parents.

Make up a Den doodle and keep record of Cub Scouts' advancement on it each week.

Paint and repair Den furniture or help make some additional pieces.

Improve the Den backyard with new games—walking rail or climbing bar.

Help some new Cub Scout get started on his achievements.

You are an older Cub Scout now. You may have some ideas of your own that would be helpful to the Den—a Den game chest might be needed, or a Den box garden, or a corner museum of leaves or shells that will catch the interest of the younger Cub Scouts. Maybe a new shack for the Den backyard, or if you have a camera maybe you could make a picture record of the Den activities.

Pack or chartered institution project — *Choose it with the help of your Cubmaster*

You can be very helpful, and at the same time bring credit to your Pack, if you serve as messenger, guide, usher, or helper at a special affair. Be in full uniform at a time like this.

Make a game or puzzle kit in a cigar box for a wounded vet. Put the name of your Pack and Den on the outside of the box. Make each piece carefully. Sandpaper the rough edges. A kit like this will be used a lot.

If your Pack's chartered institution is having a rummage sale, help out by collecting things for it in your neighborhood. Find out from your Cubmaster what is wanted.

Choose your project with your Cubmaster. He will know what needs to be done and can suggest other projects. The ones pictured on these pages are only suggestions, not requirements.

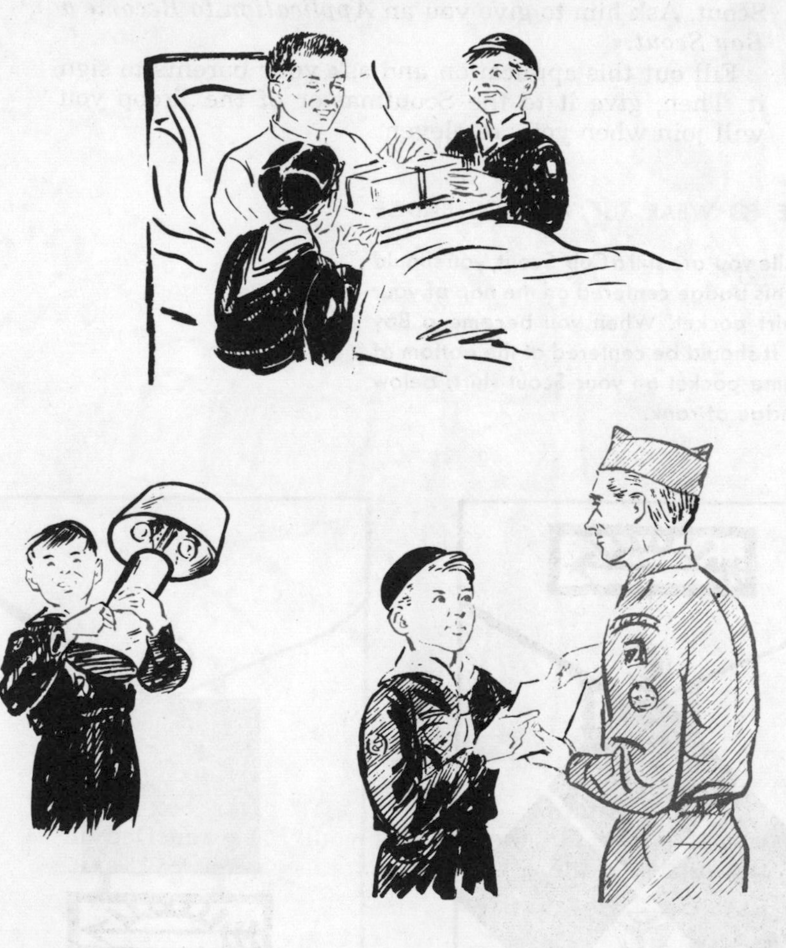

REQUIREMENTS 5 and 6

Three months before you are eleven visit a meeting of a Troop you think you'll wish to join. Maybe it's the Troop operated by the same church, synagogue, P.T.A. or group that helps you have Cub Scouting. Perhaps it's the Troop your Den Chief belongs to. Invite dad to go with you and meet the Scoutmaster.

Talk with the Scoutmaster about becoming a Boy Scout. Ask him to give you an *Application to Become a Boy Scout.*

Fill out this application and ask your parents to sign it. Then, give it to the Scoutmaster of the Troop you will join when you are eleven.

WHERE TO WEAR THE WEBELOS BADGE

While you are still a Cub Scout, you should wear this badge centered on the flap of your left shirt pocket. When you become a Boy Scout, it should be centered at the bottom of the same pocket on your Scout shirt, below the badge of rank.

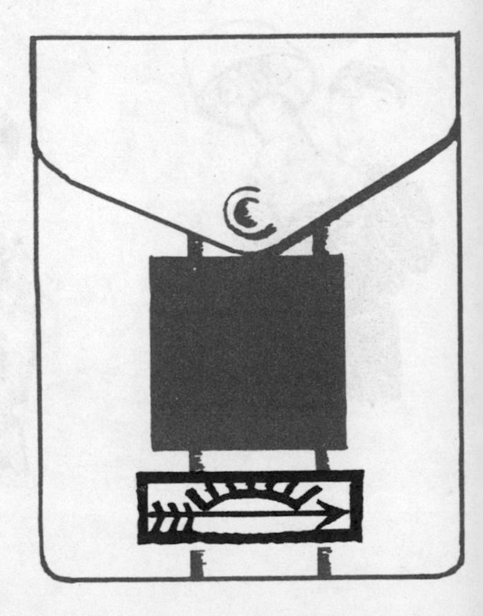

APPLICATION
TO BECOME A BOY SCOUT
BOY SCOUTS OF AMERICA

I want to be a Boy Scout. I would like to join Troop No. .... I promise to attend Patrol and Troop meetings, hikes, camping trips and other activities whenever possible. I agree to be guided by the rules of the Troop and the Scout authorities.

On my honor I will do my best:
To do my duty to God and my country, and to obey the Scout Law;
To help other people at all times;
To keep myself physically strong, mentally awake, and morally straight.

My Name ______ My Phone ______
My Address ______ My Religious Preference ______
My School ______ Grade ______ Date Joined Troop ______
My Dad has been a Scout ...... yes ☐ no ☐ a Scout Leader ...... yes ☐ no ☐
I am or have been a Cub Scout ...... yes ☐ no ☐ Pack No. ______ City ______ State ______

TROOP RECORD

Patrol ______ Fee paid ______ Registration sent to Local Council on ______ Date
Requirements completed. Candidate ______ Date Tenderfoot ______ Date

APPROVAL BY PARENTS OR GUARDIANS

WE HEREBY CERTIFY THAT ______ Boy's Name
was born ______ Month Day Year

He is at least 11 years of age or will be at the time of registration as a Boy Scout. The rules of the National Council forbid the enrollment of any boy under 11 as a Boy Scout. No ... Can Be Made. We have read the ... we are willing and desirous that ... We will try to assist him in obse... Scouts of America In consideration ... om the member-ship, if accepte... ily waive any claim against t... uncil, the Boy Scout Troop, its ... nd all Leaders of the Boy Sco... and all causes which may ar... e activities of the above Org...

Signature ______ (Guardian) ______ Address ______

As Boy Scout parents we understand that the Boy Scouting Program will be an active Program for our son, which will have many opportunities for service adventure and fun. So that our son may gain the most from his Boy Scout experience, we will cooperate:

a. By learning what Boy Scouting is and how we can assist our son and his leaders.
b. By encouraging him to take part in Patrol and Troop activities.
c. By attending events to which parents are invited.
d. By making it a point to cooperate with his leaders.

A Registration Certific... must be presented when buying the Official ... m.

Visit a Troop meeting and ask the Scoutmaster to give you an *Application to Become a Boy Scout*.

W E B E L O S

W E B E L O S

REQ NO.	REQUIREMENT	SIGNED BY
1.	Be at least 10½ years old	MOTHER OR DAD
2.	Be a Lion Cub Scout	CUBMASTER
3.	Prepared as Tenderfoot Scout	CUBMASTER

Webelos badge awarded ______________________
DATE

ACTIVITIES

PREPARE FOR SCOUTING

Well–here you are all the way through your Lion requirements and almost finished with your Webelos or maybe you have finished it and you still have a little while to go before you join the Troop. Now is the time then for you to thumb through the Elective pages in your Wolf, Bear and Lion books. You'll probably find several Electives you want to do, several things you'll want to make just for fun or for arrow credit points.

Maybe you were so busy working on your Achievements you just didn't have time to do all the things you wanted to and now with a wonderful Boy Scouting experience just ahead, we suggest that you talk over with your dad and mother the electives listed on the next page. You and your dad can have fun using the electives to help you prepare for Scouting.

S C O R E B O A R D

REQ NO.	REQUIREMENT	SIGNED BY
4.	Complete Service Project	PARENT, DEN MOTHER OR CUBMASTER
5.	Visit Troop Meeting	SCOUTMASTER
6.	Complete Boy Scout Application	SCOUTMASTER

CUBMASTER

E L E C T I V E S H E L

OUTDOOR CHEF

Lion Cub Scout Elective 19
See also Wolf Cub elective Cooking
and Bear Cub elective Party Chef

SHELTERS

Lion Cub Scout Elective 20
See also Wolf Cub elective Outing
and Bear Cub elective Shacks

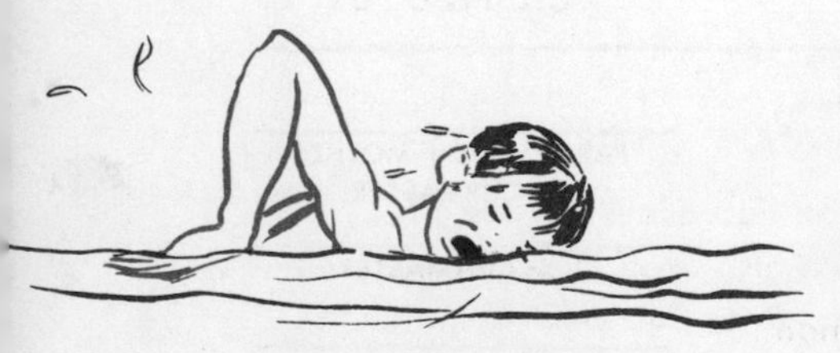

SWIMMING

Lion Cub Scout Elective 21
See also Wolf Cub elective and
Bear Cub elective Swimming

YOUR SCOUTING

SPORTS

Lion Cub Scout Elective 23
See also Wolf Cub elective
and Bear Cub elective Sports

NATURE

Lion Cub Scout Elective 15
See also Wolf Cub elective Birds
and Bear Cub elective Nature Crafts

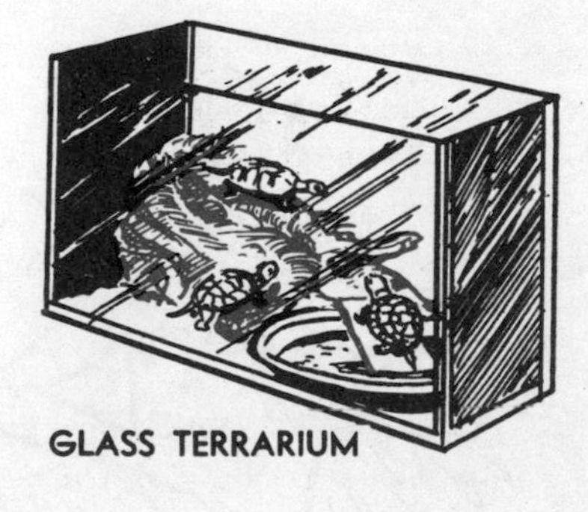

GLASS TERRARIUM

INDIAN DANCER

Lion Cub Scout Elective 11
See also Wolf Cub elective Indians
and Bear Cub elective Indian life

SWIMMING

When you go to camp as a Scout you'll have lots of chances to swim—so why not get started early?

If you haven't been swimming before, here is a dad and son project you'll have fun doing. You needn't be afraid of the water. It's the same stuff you bathe in, wash in, and drink. Now you can learn a new way to use it.

If you're just starting, try the projects on these two pages and you'll get used to the water in no time at all.

Then go on to the Swimming Elective 21. Read what it says in the *Wolf Book*, the *Bear Book*, and the *Lion Book*. You'll find some helpful ideas listed.

1. Go into the water, knee deep. Bend over, throw water over your chest and shoulders.

2. With your back towards shore, sit down so water comes up around your chest.

3. Stretch your feet out in front of you. Place your hands on the bottom in back of you. Bend your head back slightly and breathe deeply. Notice how your feet rise off the bottom. That's due to the buoyancy of water. Your legs are *floating*.

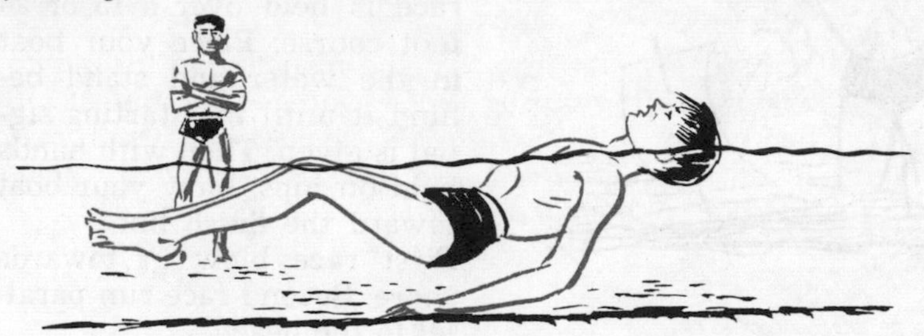

4. Now stand up and go out to water waist deep. Jump up and come down with bent knees. Notice the difference in the pressure of the air and the water around the body.

5. Stand back to back with your dad or your buddy about three feet apart and paw water back at him. It's fun and a start on using the arm stroke in swimming.

6. Another way to have fun is a shingle boat race. Point the shingles at one end. Make a hole about ⅓ of the way back from the point. Place in this hole a mast cut from the edge of the shingle. On this mast a square of paper is placed for the sail. The race is held over a 15 or 20 foot course. Place your boat in the water and stand behind it until the starting signal is given. Then with hands held on hips, blow your boat toward the finish line.
   First race blow in towards shore. Second race run parallel to the beach.

7. A crawling race is fun, too. Go to knee deep water, face shore, place your hands on bottom, feet straight back. At the signal race for shore. You can run this over a 25 foot course parallel to the beach after a while.

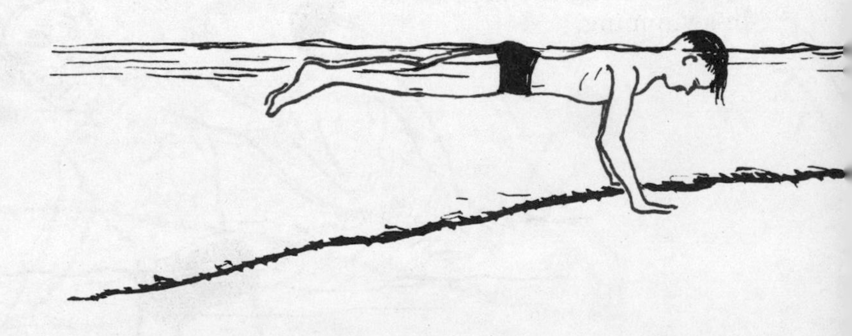

8. Many people think it is the feet that do most of the work in swimming. That is not true. The arms do about two thirds of it. You should learn the leg stroke first, however. And you can practice this at home before you go to the water. Look at the illustrations to learn how to do it.

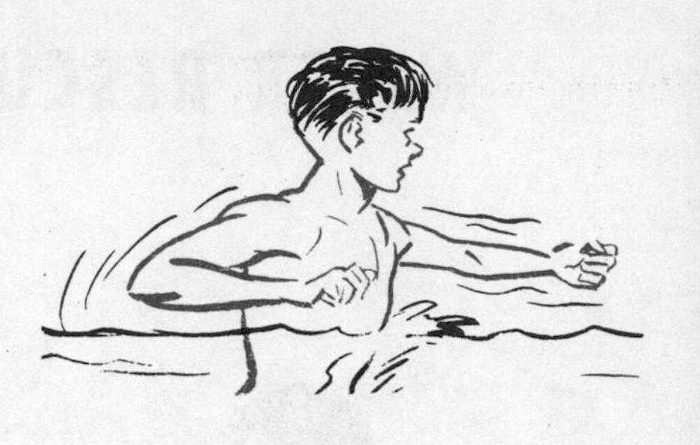

9. Stand in the water up to your lower ribs. Face your buddy who is about six feet away. Hook your toes in the bottom. Lean forward, take a breath, lower your head and plunge toward him. You will glide through the water like a fish.

WATER RESCUE

Reach by extending hand, foot, towel, jacket, pole, paddle, stick, or branch if subject is near enough.

Reach by throwing a line with or without a ring buoy attached when one is near at hand.

RIME AND REASON

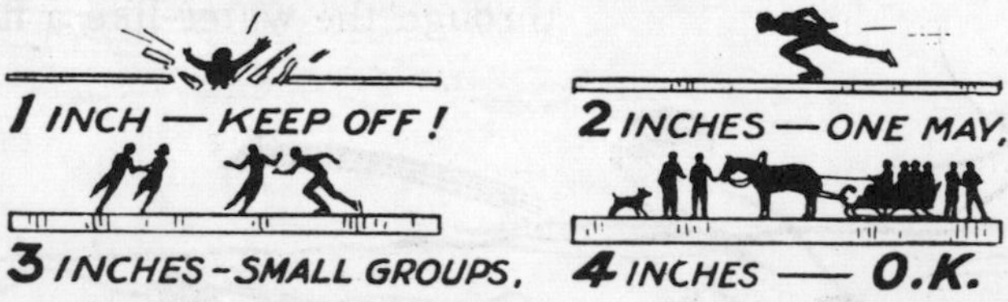

BOAT SAFETY

STEP IN THE CENTER of the boat when getting into the boat or changing seats.

DON'T OVERLOAD — seats do not indicate capacity. Two or three adults may be a full load under many conditions.

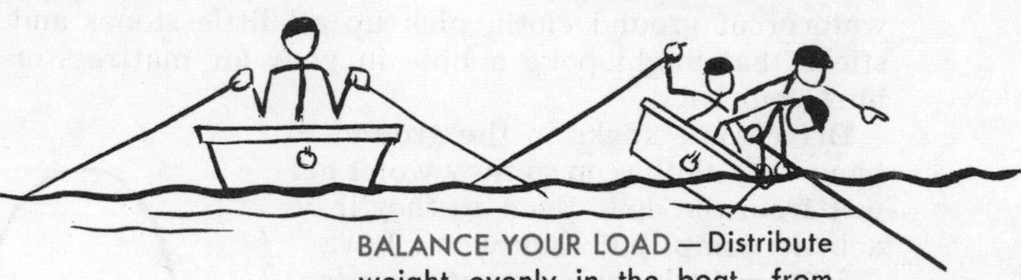

BALANCE YOUR LOAD — Distribute weight evenly in the boat — from side to side and from bow to stern.

WATCH THE WEATHER — Head for shore before a storm breaks — if caught out, seat passengers on floor.

HANG ON — If your boat or canoe rolls over, TURN IT RIGHT SIDE UP and HANG ON. Kick it ashore or wait for help. It won't let you down. If one of the party can't swim put him inside lying on bottom.

CAMP COMFORTABLY

Camping should have a purpose. Even the early explorers went out for a purpose, and camping was their means of living comfortably away from home.

Shelters keep the sun and rain off if they're made right. Here is a tab tent that you and dad and mother can make, and one you all can use on your next trip or picnic. Or you can use it in your backyard.

When you sleep out, whether you sleep on an air mattress or on the ground, go over the area on your hands and knees very carefully. Before you spread out your waterproof ground cloth, pick up all little stones and sticks that might poke a hole in your air mattress or hurt your back.

Drive some sticks in the ground to hang your clothes on so they won't get wet from the dew. Even so they'll be a little damp, but that won't hurt.

Make a little table to put your lantern or flashlight on. Don't use candles unless they're in a tin can lantern or candle holder. An open flame is as *dangerous* as it is friendly. Treat it with respect.

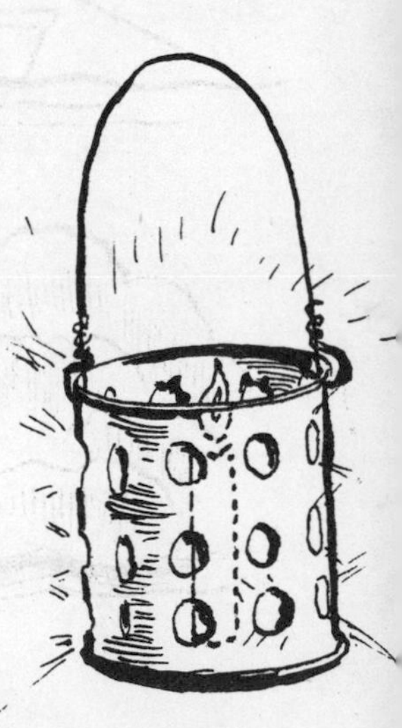

CAMP LANTERN

CLOTHES HANGERS

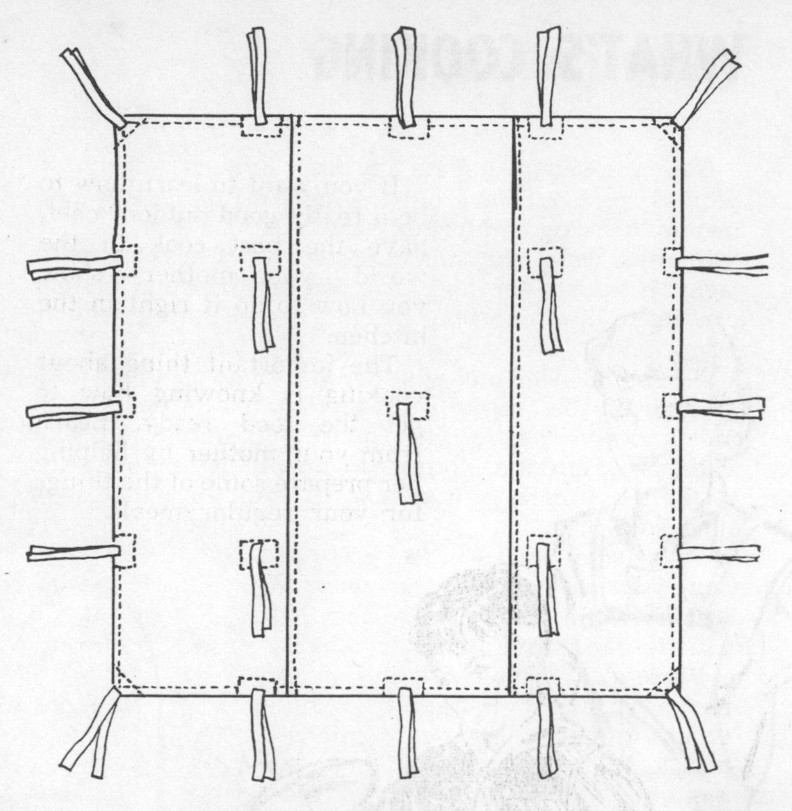

TAB TENT

WHAT'S COOKING

If you want to learn how to be a really good outdoor chef, have the best cook in the world — your mother — show you how to do it right in the kitchen.

The important thing about cooking is knowing how to get the food ready. Learn from your mother by helping her prepare some of the things for your regular meals.

Once you've learned how to fry or boil eggs in the kitchen, it's easy to repeat the process on a simple little fireplace outside that you and dad have fixed up.

You'll learn about different types of fires when you're hiking or camping with your Troop, so now let's look at some simple foods you can practice on in the kitchen and your backyard. Learn to fix them so you'll eat well even on your first hike.

COOKED CEREAL

BACON AND EGGS

HOT CHOCOLATE

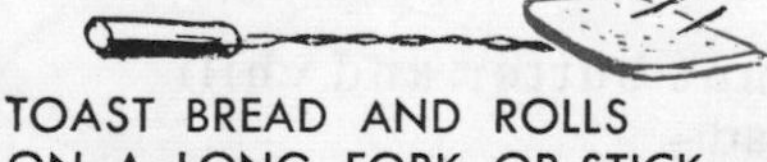

TOAST BREAD AND ROLLS ON A LONG FORK OR STICK

PREPARE HAMBURGER FOR COOKING

COOK HOTDOGS ON A STICK

OR IN WATER

COOK A CAN OF PORK AND BEANS

DEHYDRATED SOUP MIX

When you get so you can cook pretty well, invite some of your Webelos friends over for supper some night. Maybe the dads and mothers will come along, too, and you can make an evening of it.

Each one of you (dads and Cub Scouts) can prepare your favorite dish. Then put them all on the table in a real buffet style supper for your mothers.

Here are two good sandwich fillers that are swell for picnics and fishing trips. They don't dry out and they're tasty too.

1 package N. Y. cheese
1 small can tuna
Pour off oil from tuna then blend tuna with cheese and spread on bread.

Peanut butter and chili spread—

Blend together 1 tablespoon of chili sauce and enough peanut butter to make a thick creamy spread. Takes the dryness out of the peanut butter.

NATURE

While you're all together eating your picnic lunch, ask for the dads or someone to talk about wilderness manners. Some of the dads are hunters and know how important it is to leave a clean campsite.

You'll want to leave your picnic site clean, too. Place all your refuse like banana peels, paper and cans in the trash can or burner provided for them. Fires are dangerous so be sure your fire is out when you are ready to leave for home. And, leave the table and bench clean for the next family to use.

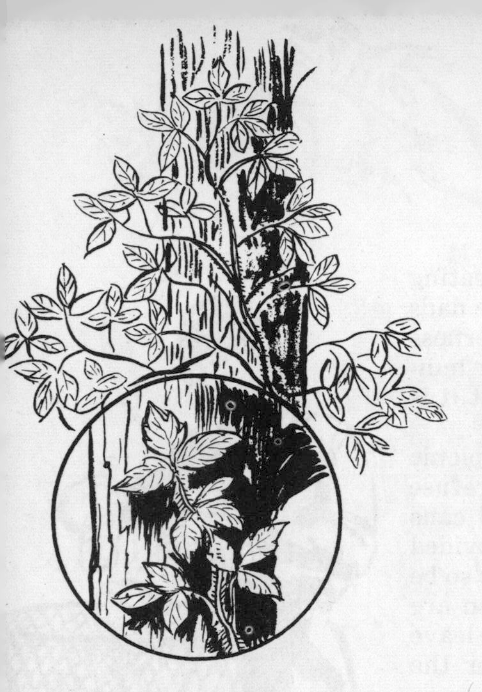

Have your dad or someone point out poisonivy to you — if it grows in your part of the country. See how many places you can find it. Notice especially the air roots that grow out from the vine as it climbs up trees and posts. Get acquainted with it, then stay away from it.

Ask one of the dads to tell you about where the birds go in the winter time.

Maybe you can all work together making feeding stations for birds.

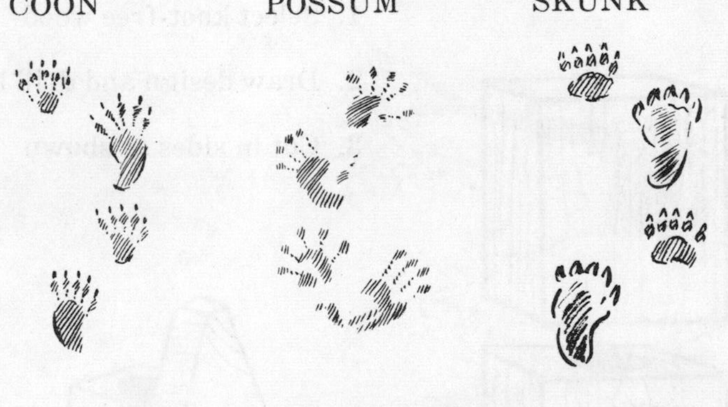

Maybe this would be a good time to make plaster casts of leaves. While you're about it, keep a sharp eye out for animal or bird tracks that would make good casts.

DAD AND SON CARVING

NECKERCHIEF SLIDES

You and dad can spend a pleasant rainy afternoon or evening making slides out of soft 1"x2"x2" pine wood. Remember the rules of knife safety. Keep your knife sharp (a dull knife slips). Keep it under control and you won't cut yourself.

Follow the steps. The wood sometimes splits when you drill your holes. It's best if your carving isn't all done if this happens.

1. Select knot-free wood
2. Draw design and drill hole
3. Cut in sides as shown

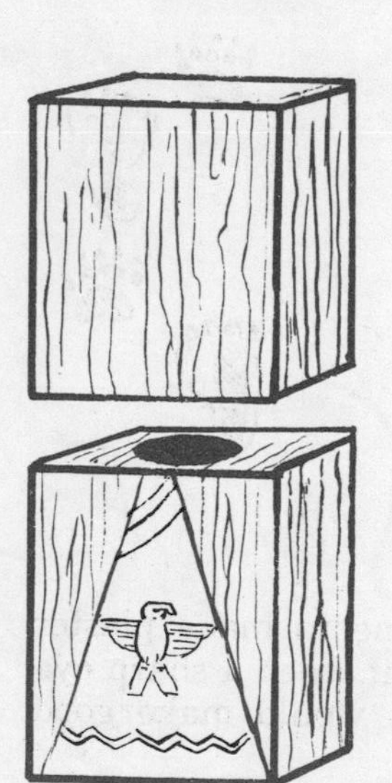

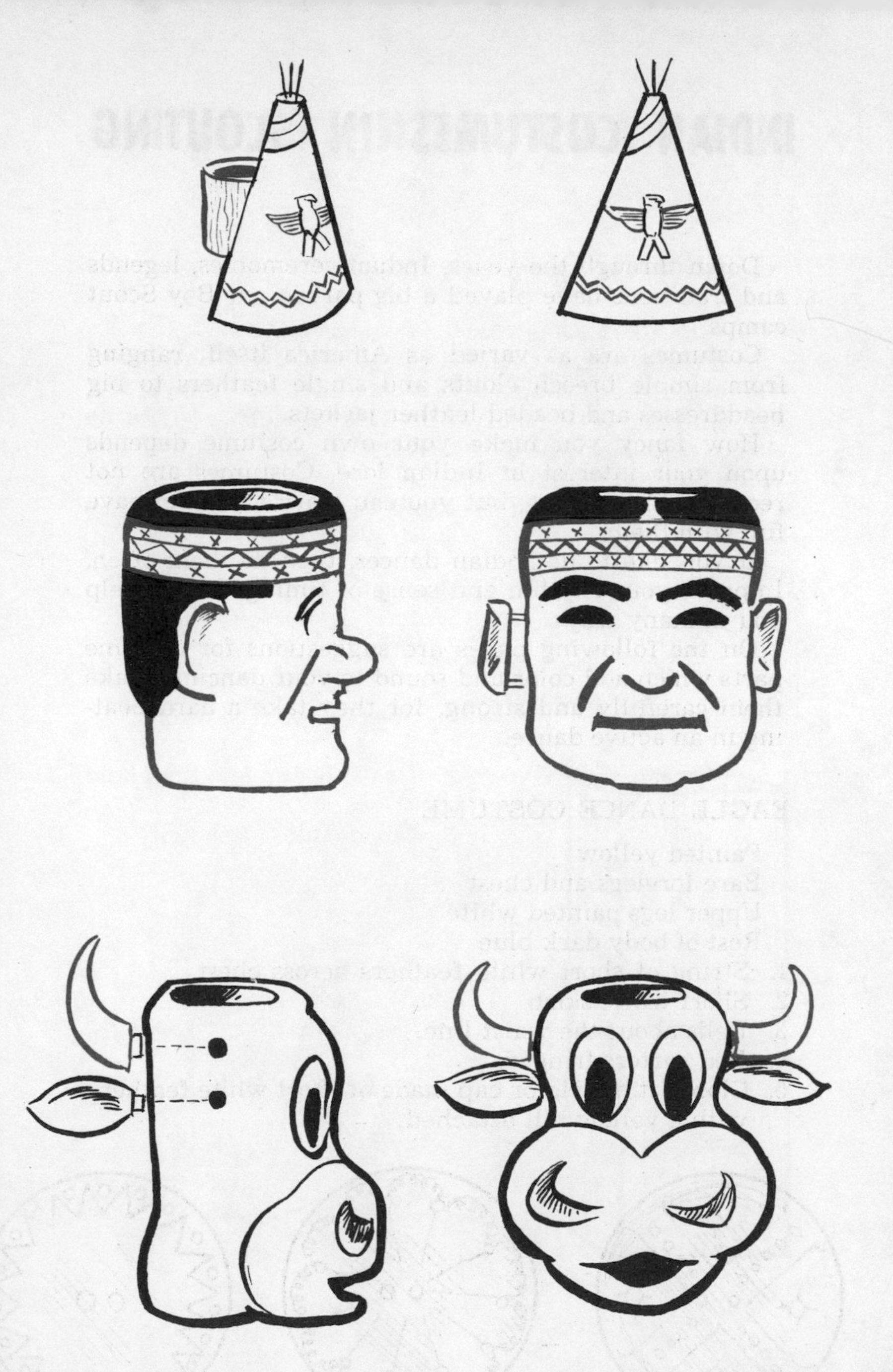

INDIAN COSTUMES IN SCOUTING

Down through the years, Indian ceremonies, legends and traditions have played a big part in our Boy Scout camps.

Costumes are as varied as America itself, ranging from simple breech clouts and single feathers to big headdresses and beaded leather jackets.

How fancy you make your own costume depends upon your interest in Indian lore. Costumes are not required in Scouting, but you can learn a lot and have fun with them.

If you like to do Indian dances, then do them often. Improve your rhythm and sense of timing. It will help you in many ways.

On the following pages are suggestions for costume parts which add color and sound to your dancing. Make them carefully and strong, for they take a hard beating in an active dance.

EAGLE DANCE COSTUME

Painted yellow
Bare forelegs and chest
Upper legs painted white
Rest of body dark blue

1. String of short white feathers across chest.
2. Short white skirt.
3. Bells about the waist line.
4. Red garters fringed.
5. Close fitting wig or cap made of short white feathers with a yellow bill attached.

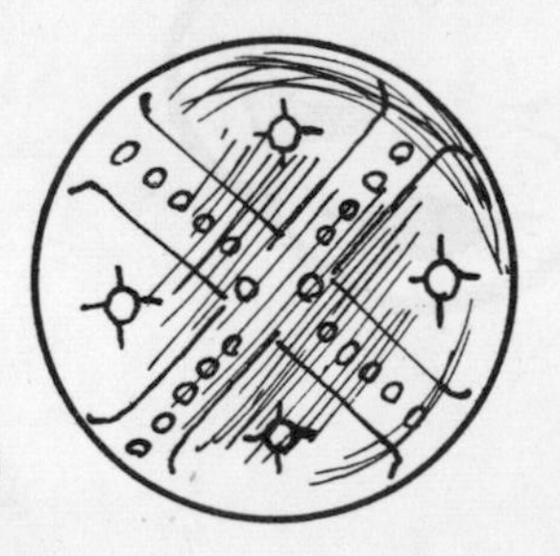

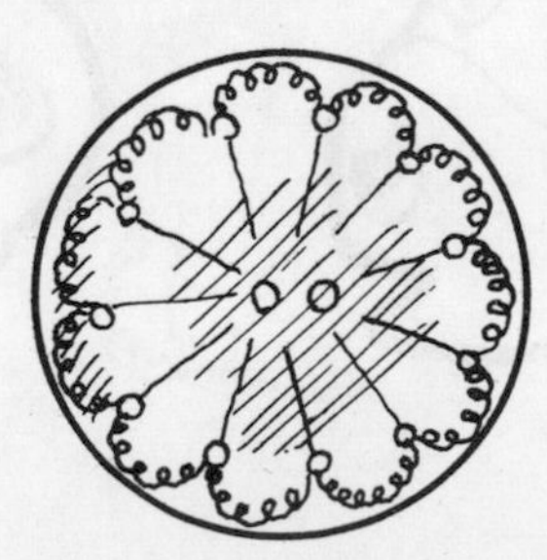

6. The wings are a strip of yellow material extending across the back of the neck along the arm line farther than the finger tips.
   To this, along the back side, are fastened the long eagle plumes hanging in a straight line.
7. Wear a dancing bustle as tail.

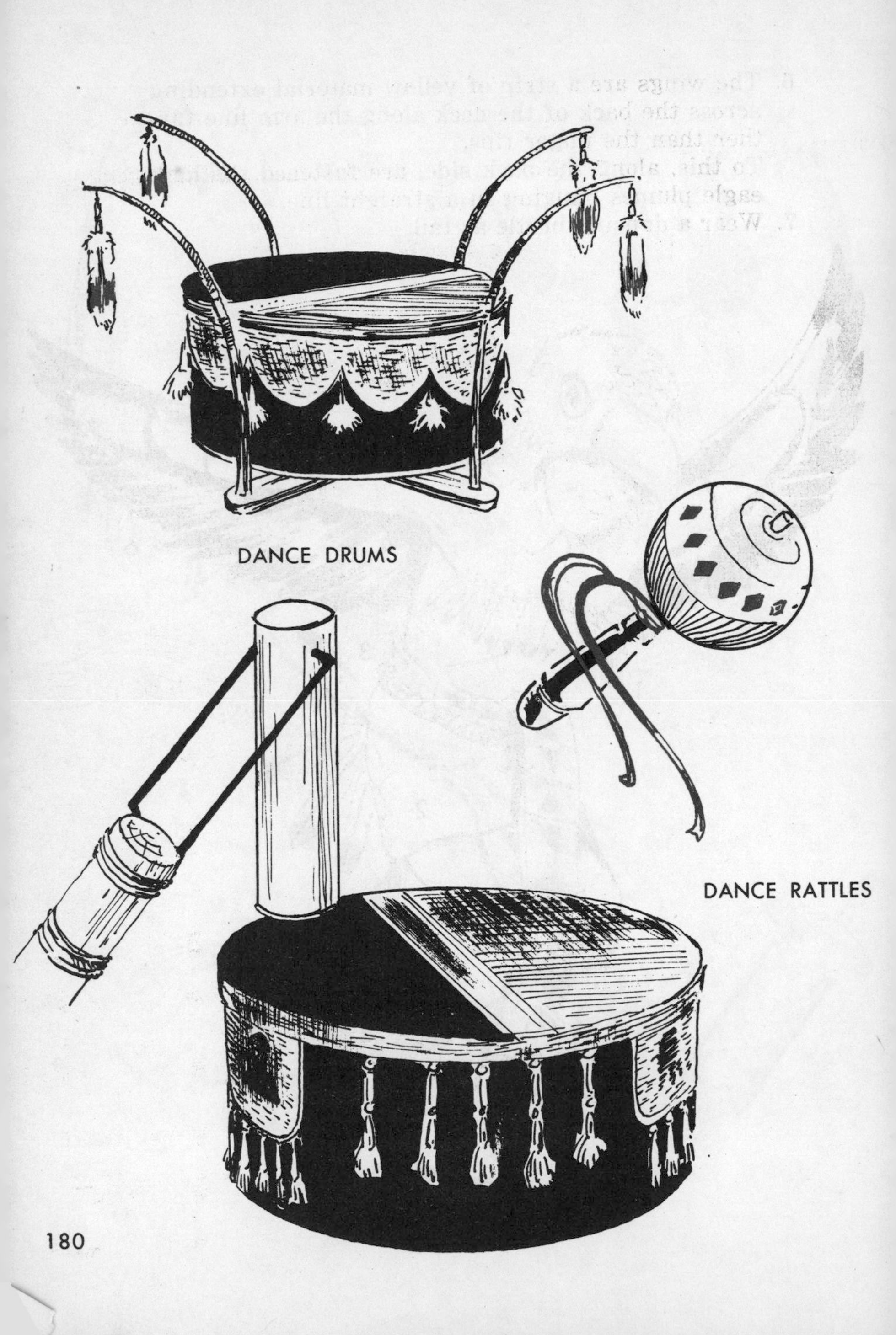
DANCE DRUMS
DANCE RATTLES

BEAR-CLAW
NECKLACE
SHIELD
DANCING BELLS
MOCCASIN
ANKLET

CUB SCOUT

MY

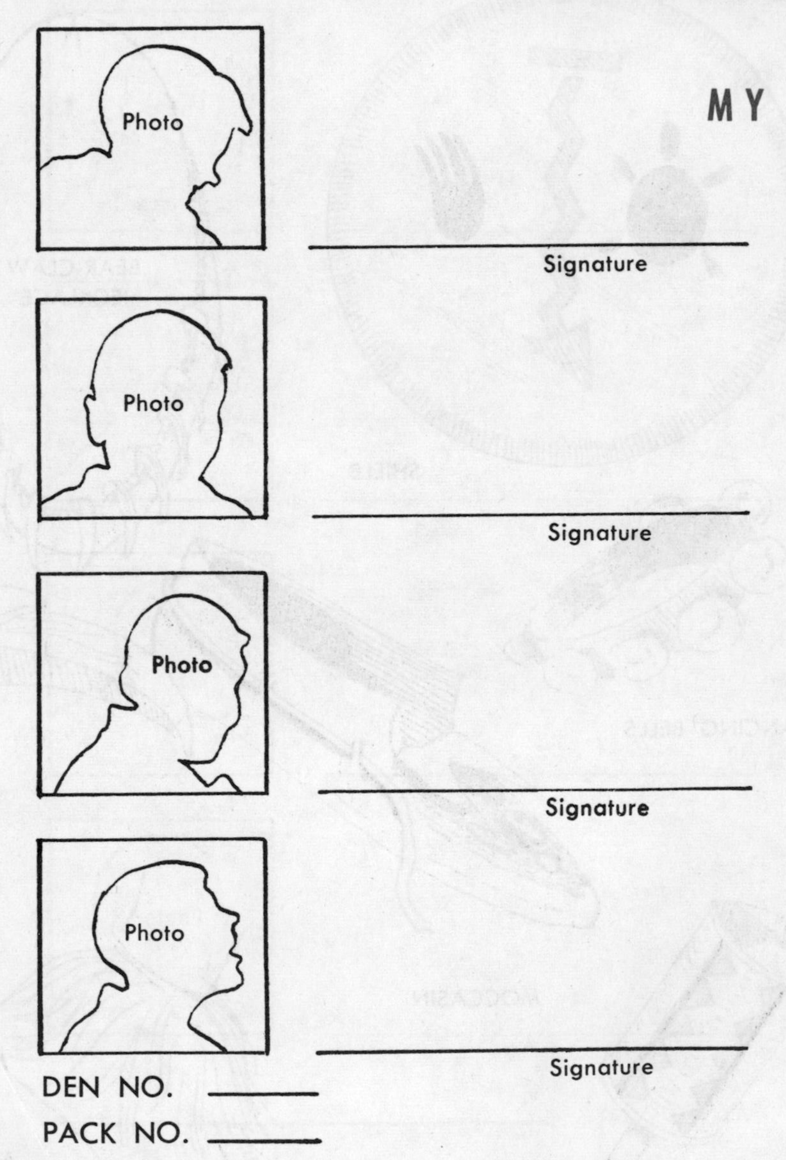

Signature

Signature

Signature

Signature

DEN NO. ______

PACK NO. ______

MEMORIES

DEN

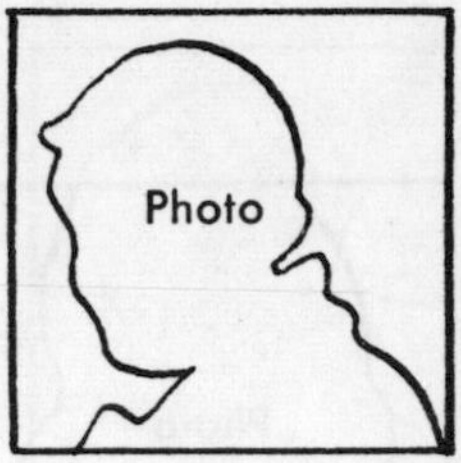

Photo

Signature

Photo

Signature

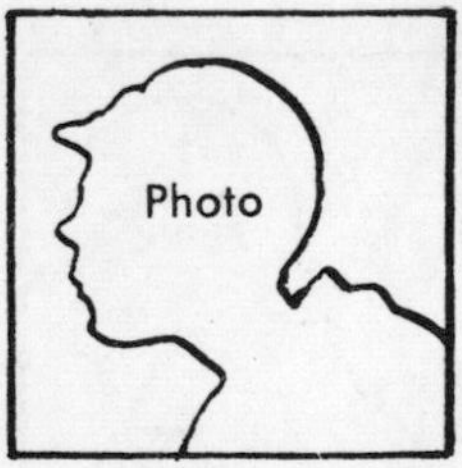

Photo

Signature

Photo

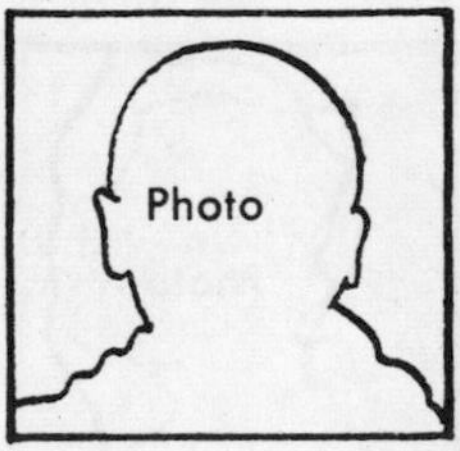

Signature

MY TOWN

CUB SCOUT

MY DEN AND

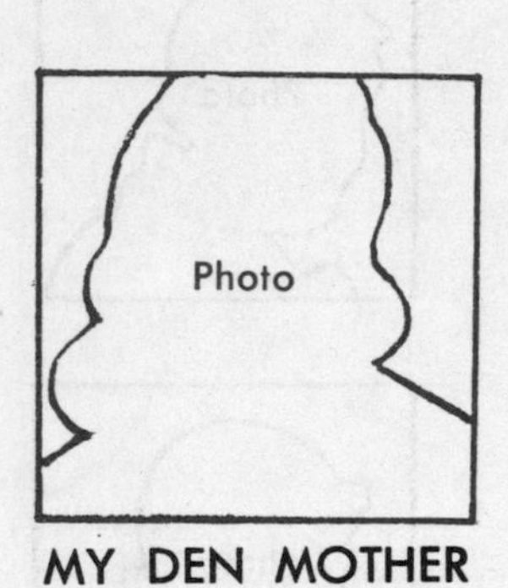

MY DEN MOTHER

Signature

MY DEN CHIEF

Signature

MEMORIES

PACK LEADERS

Photo

Signature

MY CUBMASTER

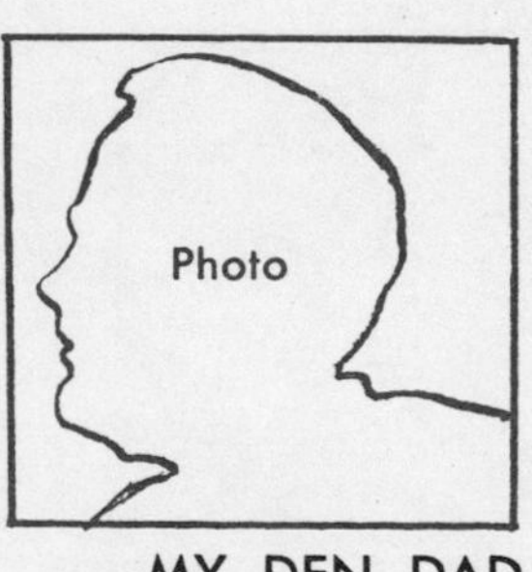

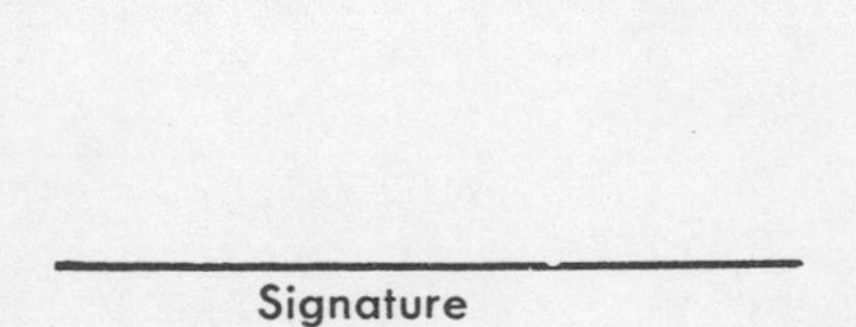

MY DEN DAD

CUB SCOUT

OUR DEN YELL

MEMORIES

WHAT WE DID

TROPHY SKIN

A trophy skin is easy to make and will look nice hanging on your wall. Cut out a piece of leather, canvas or cardboard. Tie four sticks together as shown and lace the skin to them Indian style.

You'll want to keep the badges you have earned as well as your Den numeral, Pack number, community strip, and badges of office.

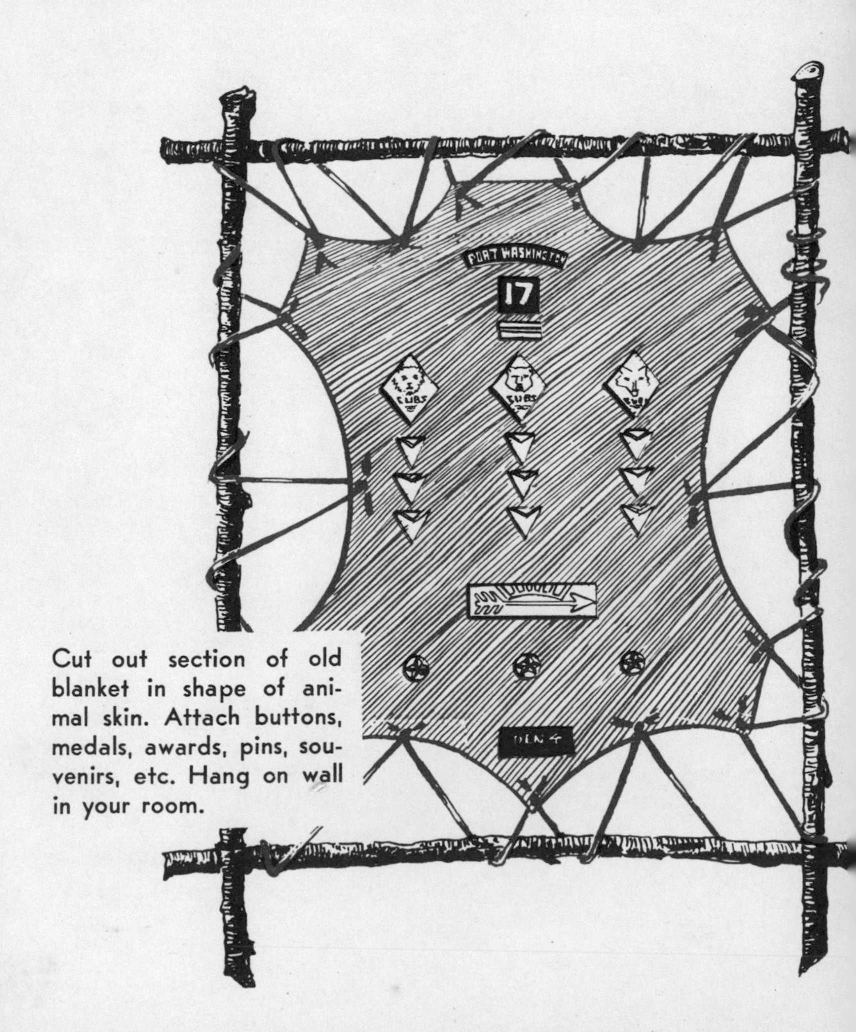

Cut out section of old blanket in shape of animal skin. Attach buttons, medals, awards, pins, souvenirs, etc. Hang on wall in your room.